Through Animals' Eyes

True Stories from a Wildlife Sanctuary

Lynn Marie Cuny

University of North Texas Press
Denton, Texas

5   4   3   2   1

Requests for permission to reproduce materials
from this book should be directed to:

Permissions
University of North Texas Press
PO Box 311336
Denton TX 76203-1336
940-565-2142

The paper used in this book meets the minimum requirements
of the American National Standard for Permanence of Paper
for Printed Library Materials, z39.48.1984. Binding materials
have been chosen for durability.

Library of Congress Cataloging-in-Publication Data

Cuny, Lynn Marie, 1951–
    Through animals' eyes : true stories from a wildlife
sanctuary / Lynn Marie Cuny.
        p.   cm.
    ISBN 1-57441-062-8 (cloth : alk. paper)
    1. Wildlife rescue—Texas–Anecdotes.   2. Wildlife
rehabilitation—Texas—Anecdotes.   3. Wildlife Rescue &
Rehabilitation, Inc.—Anecdotes.   I. Title.
    QL83.2.C85   1999
    639.9'09764—dc21   98–32109
                                        CIP

Photographs in the book are by Tim Ajax, Bill Terry,
Tom Adams and from the WRR Archives.
Design by Angela Schmitt.

To my beloved parents, Agnes Grenrood Cuny and Robert Cuny, who taught me to laugh, to love and appreciate Nature, and to follow my heart every day of my life

and

to all non-human animals everywhere who have been deprived of their birthright to a life of peace, freedom and respect as sentient beings

Contents

Preface

Since incorporating in 1978, Wildlife Rescue and Rehabilitation, Inc. has been accepting, caring for and rehabilitating injured, orphaned, abused and displaced wild animals and returning them to their natural habitats. All too often, these extraordinary wild animals are homeless and in danger, not because they have entered man's land, but because man has entered theirs. With our help, these animals are returned to their natural environments, free and healthy. Others aren't so fortunate. Severe disabilities impair their survival in nature. Thankfully, we can keep them safe and care for them in our permanent Sanctuary.

Our daily mission at Wildlife Rescue and Rehabilitation, Inc. is to preserve wildlife living under the constant threat of human encroachment, habitat destruction and death. With our devotion to the survival of wild animals and the ongoing support of our loyal members and caring community, we can continue to make major contributions to national conservation efforts. With your help and sensitivity, we will continue to make a difference.

It is time for each of us to take the steps necessary to save our planet. There may never be a time of greater global awareness or a better opportunity for all of us to work together to save Mother Earth.

Lynn Cuny
Wildlife Rescue & Rehabilitation, Inc.

The History of
Wildlife Rescue & Rehabilitation

Founded by Lynn Cuny in 1977, Wildlife Rescue & Rehabilitation, Inc. (WRR) was incorporated as a not-for-profit organization in 1978. Its purpose is to provide rescue,
rehabilitation and release of orphaned, injured and displaced
wildlife. In addition, WRR gives permanent care, in large natural habitats, to indigenous wildlife who, due to severe injuries,
have been deemed non-releasable. WRR also provides permanent care for non-indigenous wild animals who have been vic-
timized by the exotic pet trade, rescued from roadside zoos,
or retired from research facilities. Prior to the founding of the
organization, the general public was in the position of being
forced to deal with many wild animals, or rely on the services
of the police and fire departments. No entity existed that was
properly trained to humanely handle many situations involving wild animals. Squirrels who had found their way into
houses, raccoons in attics, and bats trapped in commercial
buildings are just a few examples of the many types of rescues
performed daily by this organization. WRR also responds to
calls from the public to rescue orphaned wild animals whose
parents have been poisoned, trapped, shot or killed on our
highways. With the arrival of a not-for-profit organization spe-
cializing in wildlife, new options became available to both the
public and the animals. During the first year of operation, WRR
rescued over sixty wild animals by responding to calls from
the public and police and fire departments. WRR also helped
resolve many situations involving wildlife via its twenty-four-
hour emergency hotline.

Within just three years, the number of wild animals in need of assistance increased so dramatically that WRR moved from Lynn Cuny's back yard to a four-acre site just outside the city limits of San Antonio. In addition to the increase in the number of animals rescued, donations from WRR's existing membership also increased. In 1980, the year the organization moved to its four-acre site, WRR also took in the first member of an endangered species—a female North American timber wolf.

By 1985, WRR was taking in and caring for over 1200 animals a year, including declawed bobcats and mountain lions who were victims of the exotic pet trade, orphaned raccoons, rabbits, opossums and squirrels, as well as injured hawks, owls and vultures. The four-acre Sanctuary was rapidly becoming inadequate in size and location. This fact was emphasized when a devastating flood occurred in June of 1985. It was time to move on. By the spring of 1986, WRR had received enough funding to purchase and move to a twenty-one-acre site thirty miles north of its former location.

In 1990, after thirteen years of providing large, natural captive habitats for non-releasable animals and exceedingly high standards of care for wild animals in the rehabilitation process, WRR was recognized as one of the top rehabilitation sanctuaries in the United States, and it is now one of only eighteen accredited sanctuaries in the country recognized by The Association of Sanctuaries (TAOS).

Today, the organization's number of non-releasable wild animals has increased from the original lone timber wolf to two timber wolves, thirteen mountain lions, four jaguars, three black bears and over seventy primates. In addition, WRR is the permanent home for many species of non-releasable migratory birds and non-indigenous birds who have been former "pets" and non-indigenous reptiles. WRR now rescues over

5,000 wild animals annually, provides a volunteer speakers bureau to schools and civic organizations and continues to maintain a twenty-four-hour, 365-days-a-year wildlife emergency hotline. WRR has a membership of over 7,000 individuals, a volunteer group of 200, plus fifteen staff members. In addition to receiving funding from the private sector, WRR receives funds from corporations, foundations and private trusts.

Like all accredited TAOS sanctuaries, WRR is not open to the public and the animals are never placed on exhibit. Another function of WRR is to increase public awareness—without the use of animals—through educational outreach programs which focus on wildlife protection, habitat preservation, and overall conservation of all wildlife, both free-roaming and captive.

For more information on WRR, contact:

Wildlife Rescue and Rehabilitation, Inc.
P.O. Box 34FF
San Antonio, TX 78201

phone 210-698-1709

1

A Day in the Duck Family's Life

After more than seventeen years of rescuing wild animals from every imaginable fate, I always have to remember what would have become of them had we not been there for them. Without a doubt, most of them would have perished. The question is: are we simply tampering with Mother Nature every time we save a life? Considering the alternative these animals face, I believe it is vitally important for us to rescue every wild animal we can. Faced with the continuing onslaught of relentless human encroachment—bulldozers, development, traffic, poisons, traps—wild animals don't have an easy life. In most cases, we're fortunate enough to be able to intervene in time to give the injured or sick animal a second chance at life.

Every so often, though, I find myself in the position of being a silent observer. I feel fortunate to have been given the gift of watching wild animals in their habitat as they prove their unlimited depth of feeling and innate ability to care for one another.

Nature may not always appear kind by our standards. Still, I believe that, if we watch with a non-judgmental eye, we will witness a tenderness and wisdom in all of the life that surrounds us.

Several years ago in early spring, my mother, sister, nephew and I were enjoying a sunny afternoon in Landa Park in New Braunfels. The spring-fed creeks and rivers running through the park are the perfect habitat for turtles, crayfish, frogs, minnows and several families of ducks. The animals have spent generations there in the clear, cold water, following Nature's plan of raising their young, finding food, living and dying.

On this bright afternoon, we watched a family of mallards swimming along in the shallow water. There were about twelve ducklings and Mom and Dad Duck. The babies were a few weeks old and just beginning to dive under the water with their parents. The entire family seemed happy to spend its days quacking, swimming and playing about in the water, splashing in the shallows and chasing dragonflies that came too close to the water's surface.

With Mom in the lead, the ducklings followed closely. Dad Duck kept a keen eye on his brood as he swam along behind. Suddenly, one of the ducklings encountered trouble. He seemed to be caught on something just below the water's surface. He kept trying to swim, but apparently could not free himself. The entire family swam over to see what was wrong. My nephew waded into the water, scattering the ducks in his attempt to help the struggling youngster. As he tried to free the duckling by gently pulling, we discovered who had snagged him. A large snapping turtle was a resident of the same river, and he was in need of a meal. My nephew quickly tried to free the duckling from the turtle's grasp, but there was no way the turtle was going to let go of his dinner.

It wasn't a pleasant sight, watching one carnivorous animal going about his task of staying alive, feeding on another animal who suddenly finds his life ending. But once again, I witnessed just how animals relate to and care for each other. As the young duckling struggled in the water, the father swam around and around the frantic mother as she protected her other eleven ducklings. He quacked deep and commanding calls to each of them. Finally the mother responded and assisted him in gathering all the remaining young into one place at the water's edge. For several seconds, both parents floated side by side, deciding what to do. Then, in a very deliberate action, the mother duck, with her family of ducklings near her, swam downriver away from the tragic scene.

The father duck, however, took a very different course of action. He swam directly back to the dying baby duck and stayed there, not leaving his side for one moment. Though he couldn't change the course of Nature, he also could not leave his youngster there to die alone. That loving father comforted his baby and watched him die. Even then he stayed to mourn his loss, floating silently in the water, knowing his duckling was gone.

It wasn't until half an hour later that we watched as the father duck swam slowly downriver to reunite with his family. The mother had kept all of their other youngsters together, waiting for his return. The saddened parents floated side by side for a time, quacking in unison in quiet, low tones. The surviving ducklings swam around them, but soon began to splash and play. As the parents watched, they seemed relieved that the ordeal was behind them and their family was safe again. Now it was time to move on, caring for the dependent little ducks, helping them grow and eventually sending them off to live their own lives.

Through the ages, people have worked very hard to create an image of indifference when describing the non-human animal kingdom. It has been convenient to believe that non-human animals lack so-called *human* traits, such as devotion to family members, compassion for one another, the capability to mourn the passing of offspring and mates. I have never believed that the human animal is the only species to possess these characteristics. I think it is true that we are all different. Humans from apes, apes from elephants, elephants from ants. But "different" does not translate into "less than." To me, different means exactly that: not the same. We human animals are as different from one another as non-human animals are from each other.

These differences should not make us turn our backs on the fact that all living beings feel and care and deserve respect, love and compassion. I trust that, in the generations to come, people will find that place in their hearts that has been asleep for so long . . . the place that allows us all to care for one another.

2

An Emu Looking for a Friend

One day a juvenile emu was found wandering the streets of a nearby town, obviously in need of a home.

When he arrived at the WRR Sanctuary, we weren't sure he would be accepted by the many colonies of free-roaming birds already established there. But this particular emu was not to be discouraged. Upon his arrival, we placed him in one of our aviaries to become accustomed to his new home. He spent his days looking out at the geese, ducks, chickens and black vultures, acutely aware of the fact that all these feathered creatures were in some way related to him and he to them. But he wasn't at all sure why they seemed appalled by his presence. Over the weeks, he would coo as he looked out at the passing parade of domestic and wild bird species, but he got no positive responses. Finally, the day came when we felt he was ready to roam the Sanctuary. The emu seemed most enamored with our large colony of geese and ducks. So we walked with him down to the pond where they were busy

enjoying an afternoon swim. In true emu fashion, the new
bird with the long legs did not hesitate to get into the swim of
things. Literally! He couldn't bear to stand on the shore and
watch all of his new buddies swim by. Without waiting for an
invitation, he ran to the pond, waded in and swam out in hot
pursuit of the geese and ducks. But the other birds were not
crazy about this interloper and showed no interest in stopping to get acquainted. The faster they swam away, the faster
the emu swam after them.

For thirty minutes, he tried his very best to catch up with
at least one or two ducks, at least one or two geese. But he just
couldn't keep up with a flock of birds determined to see him
as an unwelcome guest. Finally the emu caught on. He knew
the ducks and geese did not want him and would never accept
him. With his long neck drooping, he plodded slowly up the
hill to the house.

In only minutes, he caught sight of another possibility for
his new family. Peacocks! Standing majestically near the en-

trance of the Nutrition Center was our resident peacock family. As the emu approached them, he looked hopeful. Perhaps these birds would be more friendly.

The male peacock was spreading his bright blue and green tail feathers, trying his best to impress the females, when suddenly he spied the emu. Tail feathers dropping like a splintered fan, the peacock jumped straight up and cried out an alert to the peahens. One by one, they circled around the emu, jumping feet first into the air and trying to intimidate him with their big feet. Of course, compared to an emu, peacocks do not have big feet. The emu was puzzled by the dancing peacocks, but not intimidated. Perhaps, he thought, they were trying to play. That was fine with him. He'd love to have someone to play with. He began to run and chase and peck at the peacocks, delighted he had found some feathered friends who would accept him.

But in a matter of minutes there was not a peacock in sight. Without even knowing how, the new emu had frightened away every member of the peacock family. Once again, he stood alone, his long neck drooping, without a single bird to befriend him. But we knew there was still one more possibility. Standing about a hundred yards away was a large flock of black vultures.

The core of our black vulture family at the Sanctuary is a handsome group of seven who are permanent residents. They had been shot and left for dead by people who do not see the beauty in these magnificent creatures. The crippled birds have lived here for several years, roaming freely on the grounds. As

soon as the free-flying black vultures who live in the area discovered their fallen comrades, they too decided that Wildlife
Rescue looked like a good home. About seventy of them fly

down and spend most of their days on the ground in the company of the vultures who can no longer fly.

Vultures are quite gregarious. You often see them playing pick-up sticks, playfully grasping twigs in their beaks and chasing each other until everyone has finally had a chance to enter into the fun. Black vultures are also very accepting, as the emu was about to learn.

Once the peacock family had disappeared down the hill, the new emu regained his confidence and resumed his quest for a new family. It wasn't long before he noticed the black vultures playing near the bobcat enclosure. He approached cautiously, not wanting to frighten them away. But the black vultures paid little attention to the oncoming four-foot-tall bird. He was, after all, dark brown and not entirely unlike them, though he was decidedly too tall to be a black vulture.

The emu drew closer. This group of birds was not swimming away, running away, flying away or screaming in terror at his approach. Suddenly, the emu was standing right in the middle of the largest group of black vultures he had ever seen. Watching from a distance, we couldn't help but laugh at the scene: Scores of short, coal-black birds were milling about on the ground, and there—in the center—stood "the world's tallest black vulture."

The emu curved his long neck down to get a better view of his new companions. He cooed and pecked and closely investigated this strange collection of feathered creatures. He watched as they gathered around his legs. Some pecked gently at his giant emu feet; others tugged at his feathers. But not one single vulture ran or flew away or seemed even remotely alarmed. After his repeated experiences with rejection, the emu wasn't sure how to respond to this general indifference. But that didn't last long. As the tall, lanky young bird stood poised in the midst of dozens of black vultures, he watched the approach of one particular vulture whose entire right wing had been shot off. This bird was clearly unafraid. Standing under the giant emu, he first groomed his large feet, then looked up at the huge, awkward bird who towered so high overhead, and made the perfect gesture of acceptance. The crippled old vulture took several steps away and looked carefully over the ground. He selected a crisp brown twig from among the sticks lying around, picked it up gingerly in his beak and walked over to the waiting emu. The grand old bird placed this perfect twig at the emu's feet, and invited him to join the vulture clan in a rousing game of pick-up sticks. At last, the emu had found his perfect family.

3

The White Pelican

Over the years, with the help of countless individuals, thousands of wild animals in need of our help have been brought right to our door. However, there have also been those animals who were in such dire straits that we had to go to *them*.

The call came in on a Saturday afternoon from a member of The Bexar Audubon Society. During a birdwatching expedition on Mitchell Lake Wetlands, the caller had noticed a white pelican stranded in the middle of the lake. Everytime the bird tried to lift his head, his large yellow webbed foot would jerk upwards as if attached to his lower jaw.

When we learned of the bird's plight we knew we had to find a way to rescue him. The problem was that Mitchell Lake is no ordinary lake; Mitchell Lake had once been a sewage treatment area. Today it is a vast area of what are called "polders." On the surface it appears to simply be a lake, but if you attempt to gradually walk out into it, you sink into a thick sludge. Of course, the deep polder floors also prevent any-

thing other than a flat-bottom boat from traveling any distance on the water's surface. It is fortunate that here at the Sanctuary we do have an old flat-bottom boat. It is full of dents, but it will float. What we do not have are oars, however, so staff member Tim Ajax used his imagination and located two eight-foot-long wooden poles.

With the boat, the "oars," medications, blankets and nets in hand, Tim and volunteers Trevor Smith and Dana Mitzel struck out to rescue one white pelican. Upon arriving at the lake, Tim and Trevor eased off the shore near the injured bird, using the makeshift oars to slowly push the boat towards the pelican. At one point Tim tried to get out and walk to the stranded animal, but he was almost immediately up to his waist in sludge. The pelican, watching their every move, began to thrash about. He tried to swim away from his rescuers, but every time he moved, his dark yellow pouch was yanked

down into the water. His entire beak was suddenly submerged beneath the surface, deep into the polder mud. If this went on for too long, the bird would drown.

The boat could go no farther with its two passengers, so Tim and Trevor decided to see if a lighter load would help. They made their way

back to the shore; Trevor stayed on the banks with Dana to keep watch, while Tim tried to get the boat closer to the pelican so he could catch him with his net. As Tim approached, the pelican began beating his wings in the murky water. He tried in vain to escape; again and again his webbed foot slapped the black surface, pulling his head down. Finally, in only two

attempts, the bird was caught in the net. Tim reached out and pulled him into the boat.

Once the bird was safely on shore, it was easy to see what had happened. Someone had discarded a large fish-shaped lure that was equipped with two needle-sharp treble hooks. One of the hooks had pierced the pelican's flesh just beneath his right eye; the second hook had dug its way into the webbing of his right foot. He could not swim, dive, or eat in this condition. He was emaciated, dehydrated, and frightened. It would have been ideal to remove the hooks then and there and let him go, but he was too thin. He would have to spend some time at the Sanctuary.

The pelican did not like suddenly being a captive, but he was hungry, and we were the folks with the food, so he decided to tolerate us. After some antibiotic therapy, fluids, and dozens of fish, his condition improved rapidly. In two short weeks, the pelican was ready to go back home. We had seen a small flock of pelicans at the lake the day the bird was rescued. There was every possibility that this bird had companions waiting for his return.

Early on a Sunday morning, as the sun warmed the lake's surface, a once-doomed pelican sat inside his carrier looking out at his home. The carrier door was opened. The cool morning air floated gently over the bird's head and down his broad, soft back. The carrier shook as he tried to extend his large black-tipped wings. He knew that he did not have to stay inside that box a second longer. The water was only a few feet away and he had waited long enough.

The first thing out of the carrier was one very large, flat, bright yellow webbed foot. Quickly following was an even larger beak with a magnificent pouch—that soft, yellow pouch that those sharp, painful barbs had pierced only two weeks before. Now, his soft, dense white body was once again free.

As he floated out onto the lake, the pelican's firm, white tail feathers shook back and forth, splashing water all over his back. He swam slowly and deliberately towards a small peninsula. He floated gracefully around the bend in the lake. In the distance, there sat a flock of white pelicans. This was where he was headed. As he drew closer, one of the waiting birds noticed his approach. The flock was busy basking in the sun, but one bird kept watch as our pelican swam closer and closer. Suddenly, the once-injured bird rose up, standing tall in the water, flapping his huge black and white wings. In the perfect pelican response, the resident bird welcomed the now-healthy pelican back to his home, back to his life as a member of the free-flying, swimming and fishing flock of beautiful white pelicans.

4

The Buck
and the Doe

Every winter, we rescue many white-tailed deer who are
hung in fences. Tragically, their injuries in this situation are
often fatal. For every deer who is able to run away when we
cut the fence, there are dozens who fall to the ground unable
to move, a hip dislocated, a front or rear leg broken, or permanent crippling nerve damage has occurred. For an animal
who spends most of their time walking, nervously on the watch
for predators, being unable to stand and walk is simply not an
acceptable or humane way to live. At WRR, we believe the
humane thing to do in these cases is to put an end to their
suffering. In over twenty years of pulling deer out of fences,
the staff here can count on just two hands the animals who
survived. This is the story of one who did.

Many winters in the 1980s were bitterly cold. I remember
so often going out on calls in the middle of the night to rescue
frozen birds who had just fallen to the ground, still alive, but
so cold they were unable to move. A call came in early one

January morning, just before sunrise. A college student, visiting her parents, had gone out for a walk on their property. Looking down the caliche road she noticed something moving along the fence line. As she walked closer, she could see there was a deer hung in the fence. She ran back to her house and called WRR. I knew there was no time to waste. Depending on how long the deer had been hanging there, his chances of survival would not be good.

I grabbed heavy blankets, wire cutters and medications, and rushed to the site. I drove my car as close as I could without frightening the deer even more. There at the bend in the road was an old section of barbed wire fence. Dangling in the rusty barbs was a huge white-tailed buck. Now only yards away,

I looked on in awe. This was one of the most beautiful deer I had ever seen. By his scarred face, I could tell he had survived many hunting seasons. I could not bear to think that this fence would be the death of him. There was nothing to be done but cut him free, and wait to see if he could stand. The buck tensed as I silently approached. His huge cinnamon brown eyes flashed as I began to cut the wire.

In only two snips of the sharp instrument, the deer was free. His heavy body dropped almost gracefully to the frozen grass below. I backed away. The buck tried to stand. With a deep, sorrowful moan he collapsed onto the ground. He could not get up. His once strong legs would not serve him now. He could not run from the enemy standing over him.

There was nothing more I could do. Every move I made only terrified the injured deer further. I had to walk away to give him some time to calm down. I went back to my car to wait and to hope. An hour passed and the buck lay still in the grass. His soft breath rose out of his nostrils, becoming small gray clouds in the cold morning air. I decided to try once more. Perhaps if he saw me coming towards him he would try to stand. I took three or four steps in his direction. Suddenly, he looked away from me. I could hear the sharp grass crackling under the weight of someone's steps. I stopped. Who could be out here in this cold? Why didn't the buck look alarmed? He seemed almost relieved as the sound drew closer. Coming out of a stand of gnarled junipers and oaks was a tall, sleek white-tailed doe.

Quietly, cautiously, she approached the fallen buck. She paused several feet away from him. The male white-tail, his antlers reaching into the air as if trying to pull him to his feet again, was calm. The doe stopped by his side. Her soft, moist nose gently caressed his face. Her warm, pink tongue began to lick his muzzle. He lay his head on the ground. The doe comforted him, nudged him, encouraged him to stand. The white-tailed buck did not get up. For twenty minutes the doe tried to coax him to follow her, but he would not move. Finally, perhaps in frustration, she lay down beside him.

For two hours they lay there quietly, breathing in unison, looking out into the frozen pasture. I knew that the more time he spent on the ground, the less hope there was of the buck ever getting up again. Three hours passed. The doe seemed anxious; she could wait no longer. She rose to her feet, licked the male twice, then turned to walk away. The hopeless buck cried out to her. His call hung sad and heavy in the frozen air. She was going away, leaving him alone with no hope of survival. I knew now what I had to do. I turned to go back to my car to retrieve the deadly injection that would put an end to his suffering and an end to the life of this beautiful white-tailed deer.

Again I heard the buck cry out to the doe, but this time she stopped, turned around, and walked back to his side. She stood over him, looking down with a piercing gaze. He struggled to stand. The buck's front legs were strong and steady as they rose up under him, his left rear leg trembled and strained. Suddenly, slowly, miraculously, the buck was once again standing. His right rear leg was weak and quivering from the injuries. You could see in his face that he was in pain. He tried to keep his balance in spite of the injured leg. It dangled loose now, serving no purpose. He could not use it and dared not put any weight on it. I stood silently, hoping that he could stand on his own.

And stand he did. The white-tailed buck knew what he had been through. He knew that if he was to survive, he had to stand and walk. He had to be able to go with the female deer who had come to his rescue. She walked ahead of him now, stopping only to nibble on some grass and look back to see if he was following. The buck took several shaky strides, his three legs carrying his weight. He did not falter; he did not look back.

Because of a persistent doe, this magnificent deer would once again stand silently in winter's cold mornings and walk majestically through the coming seasons.

5

The Three-legged Coyote

Since the often-maligned coyote is the subject of so much bad press, it's good to show another side of this wonderful animal the Native Americans called "God's Dog." We have rescued countless coyotes over the years. Many of them had been captured from the wild to be sold as "pets"; others had been caught up in urban areas with no way out. Still others had found themselves the victims of the cruel steel jaw trap.

In early June of 1981, when WRR was still at our four-acre site in Leon Springs, an elderly couple brought in a young female coyote they found on their neighbor's property. She was horribly thin and terrified, and what was left of her rear leg was full of maggots. The couple felt certain she would have to be destroyed. But one look into those intense golden-brown eyes told me she wanted to live.

As always, the first order of business was to treat her wounds and provide her with fluids and food. I will never forget how those probing eyes watched my every move. She wasn't sure she was safe. The last thing she wanted was to be handled by the enemy.

A close examination of her completely infected leg told us that the only way to save her life was to remove the leg. There was no way around it. Surgery was going to be life-threatening, but it was absolutely necessary.

After forty-eight hours of keeping her hydrated and stabilized—all the while being scrutinized by those brooding eyes—we felt the time had come for the risky surgery. The coyote was so thin, we had to keep the sedation as light as possible. Too much anesthetic could kill her. We didn't know it at the time, but there was another reason to exercise caution. Once we had her under, we discovered that this young female coyote was going to be a mother. In an instant, I understood what her eyes had been trying to tell me all along. Now we had an even greater challenge. We had to continue the surgery to save her life, but doing so could kill her pups. We had to work quickly, complete the operation, bring her back around and then watch to see if the babies survived and would continue to develop and grow.

The following days would give us our answer. As the coyote began to recover, she seemed to accept the loss of her leg. She kept the stitches clean and didn't try to chew them out. She sat patiently every day as we medicated her. She took the food we offered and all the while, she never growled. She just accepted, watched and waited.

When day seven came and there was still no sign of complications with her pups, I started to relax. By day ten, her tummy was beginning to bulge. I was convinced that the babies were safe, but now we had to make a difficult decision. Should we set her free and let her raise her young ones in the wild with no help from us? Or should we keep her, watch as the pups are born and be certain she could care for them before we set them all free?

We knew that for the pups' sake, it would be best for them to be born in the wild. Never making any positive connections with humans is always the safest way for a wild animal to live, since the chances are that most of their human contact will be negative, and even fatal. Perhaps a compromise would be best. I decided to release her on the elderly couple's property. They had over 1000 acres, liked coyotes and—if we set it up right and the coyote mom cooperated—they could keep an eye on her.

For the next five days, we fed the mom-to-be everything she would eat. I wanted her to have every advantage. That meant to be healthy enough to raise her young and hunt for them when the time came. There was also the possibility that she had other family members in the area. If this were the case, life would be much easier for her and her pups. Con-

trary to popular belief, coyotes are caring, social animals who take care of each other.

A week had passed and there was no reason to put it off any longer. I put together a makeshift den in case she wanted to use it, and packed a week's worth of coyote dinners. We decided to set her free right in the middle of the acreage, near the couple's house, so they would be able to see her if she stayed in the immediate area. I let her go at dusk. She was familiar with the area and would have the cover of night if she felt threatened.

As this once worn down, emaciated and injured female coyote emerged from her carrier, she was now strong, fat and ready to resume her life, which had been so cruelly interrupted. She cautiously returned to her world and made it clear that she wanted no part of our interference. She sniffed once around the den, snatched two pieces of juicy raw chicken and made her way to the underbrush to reclaim her place in Nature. She did not look back; she did not hesitate. She was gone. I resigned myself to never knowing how she would manage without her leg, much less how she would raise and care for her babies and teach them to hunt.

One morning in August, just an hour after sunrise, I received a call from the couple who lived at the coyote release site. No more than twenty minutes earlier, they had been sitting at their breakfast table. Off and on throughout the night, they heard coyotes howl, but now the howling seemed closer to their home. They decided to finish their breakfast on the front porch and maybe catch a glimpse of some of the coyotes living on their property. As they sipped their coffee and looked into the morning sunrise, they saw a familiar sight emerging from the underbrush. Three adult coyotes came out first, sniffing and roughhousing with each other, more playful than usual for a group of adults. As the couple watched, still another adult coyote emerged. But this coyote seemed different. She seemed to have a bit of a limp. The couple looked on in joy and relief as the limping coyote showed herself. She was the three-legged young female they had rescued more than two months before. They were so delighted to see that she had survived they almost did not notice the three coyote pups following playfully behind their mom. The other adult coyotes stayed close to the pups. If Mom fell even a little behind in the play, they were there to help out, babysit and lend support. There in that perfect morning sunrise of a new day walked that once given-up-for-dead coyote, that brave young female who knew she had a family to raise, who would not let anything stop her, not even a steel jaw trap.

There, standing firmly on her three legs, was God's Dog, with her own pups, watching with her golden-brown eyes as she reclaimed her place in Nature.

6

The Great Egret's Flight

In our early days, before catch poles and gloves, before an ample supply of carriers, crates and bedding, most of our rescues were performed on a wing and a prayer. In fact, many of our volunteers would still agree that where there is little or no cooperation on the part of the animal, rescues are still carried out on a wing and a prayer. A particular bird and a particularly humorous "rescue" come to mind.

The call came from an elderly woman who lived with her five grandchildren near the San Antonio River. It was late winter. We were receiving calls about various species of migratory birds being found tired and grounded in the San Antonio area. There were many coots, grebes and a few small herons. All they needed was some food and shelter and perhaps a safe body of water to rest on before taking flight again.

The woman described a pure white bird who was very tall—taller than her youngest grandchild—with the longest beak she had ever seen. There was no doubt in my mind that we were dealing with an egret.

Egrets and shore birds have a very low tolerance for stress. The last thing they want in their lives is a confrontation with a human, no matter how well intentioned. This particular egret had been wandering about the neighborhood for three days. On occasion he would disappear for a few hours, probably going down to the river to feed. Then he'd return to wander from yard to yard, exciting children and terrifying cats.

As I drove to rescue the bird, I had only my trusty collection of clean white sheets and a large cardboard box. I hoped and prayed that the bird was not injured, only tired, because all too often an egret with a serious wing injury can't survive the surgery needed to save the wing. When I arrived in the vicinity of the call, it was easy to see where the egret was spending his time this afternoon. On one street there was a crowd of about seven children and five or six adults. Three cats looked down from the safety of a large mesquite tree.

I parked about a block away, hoping not to contribute to the chaos. I approached a small elderly woman who, I assumed, was the person who called me. She pointed to the center of the crowd. There, standing very tall and lean, was a calm but bewildered egret. I quietly asked the crowd to give me some room so I could capture the bird and take a closer look. I was not quite sure how I was going to accomplish this, looking so very professional with my cardboard box and sheets. But I knew the time had come to do something. I wasn't too comfortable about the fact that I had a very attentive audience. All I could do was hope that they did not try to participate in the rescue.

I approached the bird slowly and quietly. I had one of my sheets at the ready, hoping against hope that the egret would let me place the sheet gently over him, making it impossible

for him to run away. Since no one had seen him fly, I had to assume that he could not.

Never assume anything about any wild animal.

Over the egret went my flowing white sheet. For about ten seconds, I felt victorious. Then, as I slowly—too slowly—approached my patient for a closer look, the majestic great egret, under the cover of a pure white sheet, began running about the neighborhood looking much like a small child masquerading as a ghost on Halloween. He made his way from yard to yard, just ahead of me and several squealing children, who were just ahead of several larger squealing adults trying to catch the children. I, looking quite foolish, continued to attempt to catch the less-than-cooperative egret.

This comedy proceeded for about one and a half blocks, although I could swear it went on for miles. Finally, the egret slowed to a steady trot. Not that birds ordinarily trot, but apparently when they're wearing sheets on their heads, they do.

Since the bird could not see me approaching, I had just enough time and space to place my foot firmly on the hem of the sheet. This time, when the big white bird took off, the sheet stayed safely behind, under my foot. That was all he needed. He ran for about ten feet, spread his magnificent soft white wings and took to the sky.

To my immense relief and amidst the cheers of the entire neighborhood, who by this time had gathered to watch the strange event, the great egret flew effortlessly down to the safety of the San Antonio River and continued flying on a very deliberate migratory route out of town.

I'm sure that the egret had been just fine all along, and most likely would have flown away in a day or so. But one can never be too sure. When a concerned person calls, we must investigate to be sure the animal comes to no harm. In the case of the great egret, I doubt that he ever landed in any neighborhood again.

As for WRR, our audience thought we did a great job. I guess they thought the best way to catch a big bird is with an even bigger sheet. I tried to tell them we were fortunate that the egret could fly away. But all they could talk about was the big bird making his way around their neighborhood wearing a flowing, white sheet. I'm sure the great egret shares our recollection, but from a decidedly different perspective.

7

The Fox Couple

Many, many years ago, in the dead of winter, Wildlife Rescue was called to trap and rescue an injured red fox. The beautiful, auburn-colored fox had been shot and severely wounded. She fortunately had managed to make her way onto a ranch near Blanco, Texas, with landowners who were sympathetic, kindhearted animal lovers. They had been putting food out for her for about three days when they called me, and were hoping that the wounds were not serious. They were optimistic that the fox would recover without any further assistance, but as the days passed, they could see that she needed more help than they could provide.

When I arrived at the wooded property, it was just after daybreak. I was hoping to get a glimpse of the fox so that I would know exactly what I was up against. My wish was almost immediately granted. Out of the dense cedar limped a thin, bloody, red fox. I could not imagine how this animal was holding on to life. Apparently the fox had been shot more than

31

once. I could see bloody bits of flesh and large patches of exposed, torn, muscle and tendons. Surely infection had set in. I knew that this poor, small, once-healthy fox must be burning up with fever. I grabbed my net and a live trap. I hated the thought of putting this animal through more stress, more fear, and more suffering, but there was no way I could help if she remained free.

As I approached slowly and cautiously, the weary and wounded red fox gave up before my very eyes. She simply could not put up a fight. I gathered the limp animal into a large, soft blanket. As I examined the emaciated body more closely I realized that I was holding an adult female red fox. I was relieved that this was winter and not spring, when I would have been deeply concerned about leaving behind a litter of babies. But I was soon to learn we *were* leaving someone behind.

I began to walk away with her when, out of that same dense underbrush, quietly crept a sleek, healthy male red fox. I knew that this could only be the devoted mate of the dying female.

As I walked towards the car, the male fox lurked only yards behind me. I could not leave the female there to die. I *had* to take her away from him and hope that, if she could be saved and returned, he would be waiting for her. As I drove away I could see him in my rearview mirror, his keen eyes watching my car disappear down the dirt road. Little by little, he slipped away in the cloud of dust left behind; quietly looking on as his mate vanished from sight.

The weeks following her capture were surely painful and terrifying for the female fox. She was on constant intravenous fluid therapy. Her wounds had to be flushed and cleaned daily. Her fur had dried and fallen out, and much of her body was left naked and raw. She would often slip into a deep sleep and I would be certain that we would lose her. Her fever would rage out of control, and then her temperature would plummet. She seemed to be drifting in and out of death's doorway.

Weeks passed as the amazing, fragile female refused to give up her fight. Finally, on a clear morning in February, the tenacious fox lifted her head. She slowly rose to a standing position and, trembling, lapped some cool fresh water from her

bowl. By noon the next day, she was able to chew on a few small pieces of raw meat. Finally, she was on her way back to her life as a free, wild red fox. On the first day of spring, a sunny March morning, I decided that the fox who had visited death and returned to life was ready to be set free.

Her beautiful red coat would never be the same. Patches of dark, coarse fur had replaced the soft copper-colored coat. The scars on her upper legs would be with her forever. Still, her spirit had not suffered. This once-again vibrant animal was jumping and pacing in her cage, eager to get back to the business of living.

As I arrived at the ranch, I remembered the day when I had driven down the same dirt road, taking the battered fox far from her home and her mate. I remembered so well that male fox watching my car drive away, watching his life's mate disappear. Months had passed since their separation. The seasons had changed and I wondered if he could possibly have known to wait for her.

As I lifted the crate out of the car, the female began to scratch at the door. Nothing else mattered to her now. She had to get out of that crate, away from her life in captivity. I opened the door, expecting a flash of red to come darting out of the carrier, never to be seen again. I was proven wrong. As the fox stepped out of the crate, she took several graceful strides out into the

sunshine. She stood still and shook her body, from her slick whiskers to the tip of her bushy tail. Every muscle twitched, every strand of fur stood out and caught the gentle movement of the wind. She knew that her life was her own once again.

I waited for about three hours. The red fox took her time as she sniffed the familiar bushes and rolled in the hard black soil. Probably just to humor me, she took a few bites of the fresh meat that I was leaving behind for her, just in case she needed it while re-adapting to her old life.

I had given up all hope of finding her mate. So much time had passed. By now, I was sure he had decided she was gone forever and had found a new companion. I consoled myself with the thought that this strong-willed female would make her way back to her world and would also find a new mate. In time, she would raise a family and give this world more beautiful red foxes.

Noon had come and the sun was high overhead. The female fox disappeared into the underbrush. It was time for me to go back home. As I drove away, I felt a little sad. But, more than anything, I felt satisfied and grateful that what could have been a tragedy had turned into one of life's miracles.

I took one last look in the rearview mirror just as I had done on the day I had taken the injured fox away. I screeched to a halt. There, just beyond the stand of dark green cedars, stood *two* red foxes. The female with her battle-scarred coat and, standing silently next to her, the male who had watched her vanish and had decided to wait for her return. He did not seem to notice her "less-than-perfect" fur. He only noticed that she had returned to him.

Only moments later, the two red foxes disappeared into the Texas brush, back into a world that belongs to them alone, back to their life together. As if humans had neither harmed nor helped them. As if they had never been apart.

8 The Magnificent Seven

Twenty years ago, when Wildlife Rescue was still based in my home in San Antonio, I was contacted by a woman who had run over a momma opossum. She stopped and got out of her car, and was horrified to find that she had indeed killed the mother. But there were seven tiny baby opossums who had somehow survived the accident. She brought them to me, still attached to their dead mother. As I peered into the cardboard box, I saw, looking back at me, seven pairs of dark black eyes set in seven soft, gray and black bodies. Every infant was making the low barking sound unique to baby opossums. I knew these little guys might be too young to survive without their mother's care. Since opossums are marsupials, they develop and grow in the safety and warmth of their mom's pouch. (There can be as many as thirteen.) They do not suck the way raccoons and kittens do. For opossums, their lifeline is the tiny thread of their mother's nipple that each baby attaches to. The nipple then swells in the infant's mouth and firmly secures the baby to the mother. The babies remain attached until about seven weeks of age, when they become only slightly less dependent on her. I estimated that the "Magnificent Seven," as I called them, were about five to six weeks old. Therefore, they had very little chance of surviving.

All the baby opossums we now rescue at WRR are nourished via a thin feeding tube that is slowly fed through their mouths and into their tiny stomachs. This method best mimics the natural way in which opossums feed when they are in their mother's pouch. But in 1979, I was still years away from developing such techniques. In "the old days," I painstakingly fed baby opossums with an eyedropper, which took many hours and a great deal of patience. Of course, Wildlife Rescue was only rescuing about 100 animals a year in those days, not the more than 5,000 that we see today. I knew that I had my work cut out for me if I was going to save the Magnificent Seven.

I began by slowly pulling each baby off the mother's nipple. They were not at all cooperative. They fought me all the way. After an hour and a half, I finally had the last baby free of the nipple and out of the dead mom opossum's pouch. The formula was warming on the stove. With my one plastic eyedropper in hand, I began to feed the little orphans. For the first several feedings, they spat back everything I tried to give them. These guys wanted no part of the eyedropper or my special formula. They just wanted their mother and all the warmth and safety that came with her.

By noon the next day I was about to give up; should I just euthanize the entire litter? Surely this would be better than slowly starving them to death and trying to force them to eat. It was late afternoon and I was at my wit's end when I gathered up one of the babies for a last-ditch effort. If this was not successful, I knew my only other alternative was one I did not want to face.

I chose the smallest of the litter, hoping he would be the most anxious to eat. I cupped the tiny body in my hand. Those huge black eyes and those soft patent leather-like ears told me that, somehow, this just had to work. I gently pressed the eyedropper to the baby's lips. He jerked away, still not impressed with what I had to offer him. I tried again. I let just a drop of formula collect on the tip of the dropper, and offered it to him. The tiny pink nose began to twitch and those coal-black eyes looked curiously at my fingers. In just one swift moment, the orphan stretched out his tongue and began to lap at the drops of fresh warm formula.

I was amazed and relieved. It took only seconds and the entire contents of the eyedropper was empty. The reluctant opossum was sitting in my hand and looking for more. Suddenly, I could not fill the dropper fast enough. I collected more liquid and went back to the same baby, who was anxiously awaiting my return. Ten eyedroppers later, the young opossum was fat, quiet, and happy. I placed him back into the box with his siblings, the fresh scent of food on his little opossum lips. The remaining six babies were very curious indeed about this wonderful new smell. Suddenly, the seventh baby was surrounded by his six brothers and sisters, all of them sniffing and licking their tiny brother's lips. Now was the perfect time for me to introduce each baby to the new concept of eating from an eyedropper.

More than two hours later, all seven baby opossums were content and sleeping peacefully in their cardboard box nest. In the coming weeks, most of my days would be consumed with administering to the needs of the Magnificent Seven. They all adapted well to using the eyedropper. They were curious and intelligent, and all had a strong will to live.

Two months later the seven opossums began to investigate the possibility of eating solid food. I started by introducing bananas, grapes, mealworms, and crickets. One by one the little opossums took a bite, sat, and slowly chewed, smacking their lips in true opossum fashion. The Magnificent Seven were well on their way to being self-sufficient, juvenile opossums.

By the end of that summer, they were all fat and sassy and ready to resume their life in the wild. I remember the night I

set them free, watching quietly as one by one they climbed into the highest branches of a giant oak tree. The whole opossum family was sniffing and licking the bark, looking for insects, and enjoying their new surroundings.

I never saw the Magnificent Seven again, but every year when I watch the hundreds of rescued opossums make their way to Wildlife Rescue, I am reminded of my first litter of helpless baby opossums.

9

The Fox
and Flora, the
Guardian Hen

If there is one thing that I have learned over the years, it is that you can never and, in fact, *should* never judge a book by its cover, a person by their actions or a situation by the way it initially appears. I am often asked whether I hate people who are cruel to animals. My response is always the same: If you hate people then you will probably find it difficult to genuinely love animals.

Though it is not always easy to remember, human and non-human animals are caught here together in the same web. We humans seem to forget that on a pretty regular basis. Our non-human animal neighbors, I suspect, have never forgotten it. One of the greatest gifts of this work is that daily, I learn another lesson from an animal.

It was the dead of winter in South Texas: cold, damp and not a leaf could be found holding fast to any tree. The fur on the wild animals was thick and soft. It was a perfect time,

41

some would say, for trapping. According to the elderly gentle-man rancher on the other end of the telephone line, he had set his trap only two days ago. Not just any trap, mind you, but a steel-jaw, leg-hold trap. The trap was to catch a fox who had been coming a little too close to his henhouse.

When he checked the trap that morning, there was a small fluffy red fox caught by the leg. The rancher did not want me to save the animal. In fact, he said that when he checked the trap the fox was still squirming, so he had remedied that with one quick blow to the fox's head before releasing the trap from her twisted leg. Now the fox lay still next to his chicken coop.

The problem was with one of his favorite hens, Flora (who had a twin sister named Dora). She was perching comfortably on the fox's body and would not leave her post. The rancher simply wanted some advice on whether he should insist that Flora vacate her now favorite roost. I suggested he leave Flora

alone for the day and that she would probably move on her own.

Flora kept her vigil through the night. At sunrise the next morning, the rancher decided he had waited long enough. Determined to change the hen's mind, he walked over to Flora and stooped down to nudge her off the body of the fallen fox.

In only a moment, the man jumped back—he knew that chickens do not growl! While Flora Hen stood her ground, the fluffy, groggy red fox turned a bright but swollen eye upward to stare at the trapper, who now cast a shadow over the fox and his strange new champion.

The rancher was aghast. "What should I do?" he shouted into the telephone. Surely, he thought, Flora was in great danger. He wanted to shoot the fox but knew he could not do so without endangering his beloved hen.

I asked him if he would consider seeing the situation through Flora's eyes. Certainly *she* was not afraid. In fact, she seemed to be protecting the fox. The gentleman simply could not understand why Flora would behave so strangely.

I suggested that he take the fox a bowl of water; I promised him that we would send someone to rescue the fox and release her far away from his property if she survived.

Still in a state of shock, he agreed to offer the fox a drink. The bowl of water was placed just in front of her small face. The fox never took her eyes off the rancher. Flora gently hopped off the fox and began to drink from the bowl. The fox waited her turn. Once Flora was through, she repositioned herself on the fox's body and only then did the fox stretch her neck out. Slowly, her dry pink tongue lapped the cool liquid.

Two hours passed. The fox began to look around, to sniff the air and try to stand. The hen once again hopped off the fox's back, but would not go far from the fox's side.

As the red fox slowly rose to her feet, Flora froze in place. She stopped pecking about in the grass, and watched as her companion struggled to regain her balance. The gentleman who had trapped the fox looked on in amazement. Though his heart could not understand what he was witnessing, he knew he had to respond.

The rancher decided to let the fox stay on his property. He had become fascinated with the friendship developing between the fox and the hen.

He tossed a small piece of meat to the fox, who wasted no time accepting his peace offering. The fox and Flora took several steps together to a spot where the leaves were thicker and not so damp. There they bedded down. Flora, determined and loyal, lay close by. Often, she nestled in the fox's beautiful fur, helping to keep them both warm. The rancher provided them with food and water: meat for the fox and grain for Flora. The fox kept a close and wary eye on him, but always accepted the rancher's hospitality.

That evening, a cold rain fell from the night sky, but still Flora would not abandon her watch. Four days passed. They had been cold, gray days. On the fifth day, the air was crisp and finally the sun was shining. Flora was resuming her chicken-like behavior, hunting for insects and gingerly picking up the seed that was scattered on the ground. The gentle red fox was able to stand, to stretch her legs, and to walk with a slight limp, despite her injured leg.

Flora had been sitting next to the fox all afternoon. That evening, she pecked at the fox's long coat, scratched in the leaves that had been their bed, then turned away and headed for the hen house.

The fox was alert as she watched Flora disappear into the group of hens who were all settling in for the night. Then, as if waiting for just the right moment, she shook her head and let the cool night air course through her fur. She gave a quick glance to the man who had once been her captor and, in one perfect fluid motion, she disappeared into the night. She was never again to venture near the rancher, his hen house or her strange companion, Flora, the Guardian Hen.

Rescued from the Dark

Not long ago WRR was called on to rescue a young mountain lion who had been abandoned in a deserted house. There were empty cans of food scattered around this darkened room and she had no water. The odor of urine permeated the room. A shredded mattress was her bed. Fortunately, she had a shrill cry that carried far enough for the neighbors to hear. Not knowing what the sound was, they called the police.

When WRR's Tim Ajax arrived at the house, he realized that the only way to safely remove the mountain lion from the room was to tranquilize her. This was no easy task because she was trying to claw her way out through the keyhole in the door and, with the lack of light in the room, it was almost impossible to see her. Regardless of all of the obstacles, she was in need of our help and Tim was not about to leave her there.

The only way to reach her was to go into the room. The cougar did not know Tim and he did not know her. Neither was quite sure what to expect.

Once he was inside the room, the young cat did her best to hide under a small table or crouch behind an empty cardboard box that was lying on the filthy floor. She had no reason to be anything but terrified of this new intruder. Finally, Tim was able to dart her. Once tranquilized, she slowly began to calm down. Now she could be placed in a carrier and safely transported to the Sanctuary.

When she arrived, of course, she did not know where she was. She was anxious and hungry. She had been living in total darkness but was now surrounded not only by light, but scents and sounds as well.

The young cat was curious and acutely aware of the fact that she was in a new world. She was also aware that there were other cougars in this new world. People who breed mountain lions to be sold to the public deprive them of their mother's care when they are only weeks old. After she was taken away from her mother, it is unlikely that she had ever been in the company of other mountain lions. She was about to be introduced to a brand new family.

The young mountain lion cautiously stepped from the carrier into the bright sunlight. Startled, she quickly lunged back into the crate—back into the darkness in which she had been forced to adapt. Several minutes later she decided to try again. Now only two steps out of the box, there was soft green grass under her feet, and a cool breeze carried the scent of our other thirteen mountain lions to this new female cougar. Her bright eyes darted about. Her ears picked up each purr and growl

that were the greetings from our resident cats. As she bravely strode out into her new enclosure, any fear she had was overcome by curiosity about her new surroundings. There were cedar and oak trees to climb, a deep pool filled with cool, fresh water, wildflowers blooming all around her, and best of all, there was this strange new, warm bright light overhead. It was the sun, the huge yellow light that

must have all but faded from her young cougar memory. It was warm as she let its light melt into her body and touch every muscle, every fine strand of her caramel-colored fur.

She was a cougar again, a mountain lion, a natural predator who had miraculously found her way back into a slice of Nature; back to a piece of the world from which she should have never been deprived. She was home. It was not the perfect home—not freedom to run for miles and miles or to stretch out on the tops of rocky cliffs and survey a cougar's real world—but a home, nonetheless. Here there was grass and fresh air and that wonderful warm sun. Never again would she have to spend her days locked in a house, secluded behind boarded-up windows. Little by little, the female cougar met her new companions. Slowly and gently they touched noses. A cautious lick of affection from one of her own kind told her that she was safe at last. From now on, there would be plenty of food, fresh water, and companions.

Our young mountain lion is one of the more fortunate ones. Hundreds of mountain lions are bought and sold throughout the state of Texas every year. They are exhibited on cement slabs in roadside zoos. They are chained to trees in backyards to serve as guard animals. They are locked up in houses, exhibited at carnivals, and hunted year-round. They are trapped, poisoned, skinned and mounted.

This beautiful animal, this precious, mysterious, secretive, misunderstood, irreplaceable and majestic cat is being systematically removed from our state. One by one, we are losing some of the most beautiful animals in Texas because there are no laws to protect the cougar in his and her natural habitat.

The mountain lion is known by many names. Cougar, cat-a-mount, puma, American lion, panther, and ghost cat. Let us do all that we can to ensure that "Extinct" is never one of these names.

The Vulture's Flight

Several years ago, when WRR was located at the four-acre site near Leon Springs, we received a call from a man who had found a large injured black bird in his field. I asked him if the bird was a grackle. He wasn't sure what a grackle was, but he said it seemed likely that this was one. I asked him to cover the bird gently with a towel or pillowcase, place her in a box and bring her to the Sanctuary. The man replied that all he had was a minnow net and he would do what he could with that.

Within the hour, an old blue pickup truck arrived in our driveway. The man stepped out of the truck and said, "Lady, I've got your grackle." I immediately went to the back of the truck and opened the camper door. There, sitting with a minnow net draped like a mantilla over her head and down to her very large feet, was one very disgruntled black vulture. She cocked her head and looked up at me as if to say: "Please tell this gentleman that I am *not* a grackle!"

Once I removed the tangled headdress from the vulture's body, it was easy to see that someone had used her for target practice. Whoever had shot off most of her right wing had also left her for dead. The wound was infected, and the bird was quite emaciated and dehydrated.

Once we cleaned her wounds and medicated her for the infection, it was time to find our new patient something to eat. Contrary to what most people think, vultures can be picky about their diet, especially in captivity. But this vulture was not interested in being picky. She was interested only in eating. After consuming a huge platter of fresh meat, she was ready to sit back and rest.

For the next several weeks, we kept her in a large flight cage. Even though she could no longer fly, she did enjoy climbing about the tree in her new home. It wasn't long before she adapted to life without flight. She had developed a remarkable way of getting into the very top of the tree. She would use her beak and feet the way a parrot does and climb to the heights of the tall oak.

One day, I decided to let her out of her enclosure to walk around the Sanctuary grounds. Since the property was completely fenced, she would be safe. After about an hour, the vulture was nowhere to be found. We looked everywhere . . . except up. This amazing bird had climbed to the top of the tallest oak tree, which grew just outside the back door of the Sanctuary house. At the foot of the tree was a large pool for the ducks. There was no doubt about it. The black vulture had chosen her new home.

Every morning, she'd climb down from her tree, wade in the pool, often right alongside the ducks, then have her breakfast of fresh meat before returning to her lofty perch. She would often come down in the middle of the day to play her game of pick-up sticks: running around and gathering up small twigs, carrying them over to the side of the pool, dropping them in one by one, then dancing around them with her wings spread. She would entertain herself for about

an hour before jumping into the pool and splashing about.

It was a joy to watch this beautiful black bird come alive again and make the best of her less-than-perfect situation. Little did we know that she had not seen the end of her days in the air. On April 1st of the following year, our black vulture was to have one more grand flight.

The day started out as most do. There were babies to feed, dishes to wash, phones to answer, animals to rescue and treat. Everything was normal . . . except that at approximately 2:00 in the afternoon, a severe storm warning was issued for our area. High winds and heavy rains were predicted. Preparing for the worst, we had all the animals in sheltered areas by noon. All the ones living in enclosures were secured. The free-roaming ducks and one large black vulture were finding their own shelter and weren't interested in any man-made protection. As it turned out, the weather forecasters were half right. There wasn't any rain, but there were very high winds of seventy miles per hour. I do not remember actually watching the wind sweeping anyone into the sky, but the trees bent down to the ground and a blinding dust filled the air.

When everything finally quieted down and it was time to survey the damage, there was only one real noticeable difference. We were missing one black vulture. She was not in her tree. She was not on the ground. She wasn't anywhere to be found on our four acres.

I called volunteers to form a search party. We put up signs as far as five miles away and notified store owners, residents, newspapers and anyone else we could think of.

Day one passed with no word. Days two, three and four passed and still no sign of our precious vulture. By day five, I had decided that, after being blown away in the storm, she must have landed so hard she had been killed on impact. The only consolation was that perhaps in the moment of becoming airborne, she felt once again united with the sky, the very place that used to be her home.

One week after she disappeared, I was at the Sanctuary, standing at the back door, talking on the phone. Out of the corner of my eye, I saw something dark by the gate, which seemed to be moving toward me. I thought it was a garbage bag blowing in the wind. When I finally looked up, I was thrilled to see that the garbage bag was actually one extremely exhausted black vulture!

This remarkable bird barely noticed me. She trotted by, intent on her pool. As she hopped in and cooled her feet, she had the most relieved look on her face that I have ever seen on a bird. After being blown away, she managed to find her way home once again, tired and hungry.

For years after her final flight, the black vulture, now living at the Sanctuary, has spent her days with other flightless vultures, sitting in the tops of trees. One thing still makes her unique. Every time the wind picks up, she comes down from the tree, sits quietly on the ground, and waits for the danger to pass. I feel certain that neither of us will ever forget her exciting adventure.

12

Love at First Sight

In 1983 WRR received one female kinkajou who had been a "pet" for thirteen years. Her "owner" had cared for her for all those years and finally reached a point where, because of her typical wild animal behavior, she had to give her up. A special enclosure, twenty feet tall, thirty feet long and twenty-one feet wide, was constructed for her at our Sanctuary. There were oak and cedar trees growing throughout the enclosure, and several sleeping boxes placed near the top gave the kinkajou plenty of climbing space.

Kinkajous are in the same family as raccoons, and consequently our new resident became the official welcoming committee of one for all incoming raccoons. For the next three years the female kinkajou cohabited with hundreds of young raccoons being rehabilitated and readied for release, as well as injured raccoons staying with WRR just long enough to recuperate from various injuries. Always she was the perfect hostess, sleeping with and often grooming the visiting coons.

Though it was comforting to see her in the company of a distant relative, we always knew that for her it wasn't quite the same as having another kinkajou around.

In April of 1988 WRR received a call from the Louisiana SPCA, as well as the Audubon Zoo in New Orleans, that a young male kinkajou had been found roaming the streets. He was malnourished, unclaimed by anyone, and in need of a good permanent home. Needless to say, our immediate response was "send him over!" Once again Southwest Airlines came through for the animals, flying the kinkajou from New Orleans to San Antonio free of charge. Once we had him in our care, we could see that the new permanent resident was young and healthy (if a bit thin).

Once he was neutered, the next order of business was to get him through the quarantine period. Soon after, the new kinkajou was placed in an enclosure near the female, so they

could get acquainted without actually being together. For two weeks the kinkajous watched and sniffed and called to each other from a distance. On May 31st, early in the evening (kinkajous are nocturnal) the male was placed in the female's enclosure. He immediately poked his head out of the carrier to observe his new home. Seconds afterward the female came down from her treehouse to discover that no, this wasn't another raccoon passing through, but a kinkajou; one of her own kind!

The kinkajous touched noses in instant recognition. Then the male gently grasped the female's head in his hand and buried his face in her neck. At first, she was a little surprised. But she obviously enjoyed it when he began grooming her from head to toe. After several minutes of chirping and touching, the two kinkajous headed for the treetops where they engaged in an all-night game of chase, bounding from tree to tree, each thrilled to be with the other.

13

Hope Comes to Syra

Many years ago, Wildlife Rescue was asked to rescue a young black bear from a zoo in Syracuse, New York. Syra, as she was called by her caretakers, had been orphaned when her mother was killed. She was also forced to suffer the cruelties of a roadside zoo before finding temporary sanctuary at the Burnet Park Zoo in Syracuse. Because the Syracuse Zoo didn't have room to keep her and because she had been declawed by her previous "owner," she could not be returned to the wild. Syra was one tired, lonely little bear cub when she arrived. She had been accustomed to living in close quarters at the zoo and to receiving a great deal of personal attention. Here, in her new home, she was a bit overwhelmed by all the wide open space of the bear enclosure, and somewhat disappointed to find she was no longer the center of attention. It was quite clear that we had to find her a friend.

Barely two weeks after she arrived, we received a call from the Parks & Recreation Department of Kingston, New York.

They wondered if we had room for a young female black bear cub living in less than perfect conditions. After much red tape and countless phone calls to city officials, the way was paved for the second black bear cub, whom they called Hope, to meet her new roommate.

Hope arrived late on a Friday night and was not thrilled with her new home. In fact, she did her absolute best to climb to the very top of the enclosure and test the fencing to see if it would give way and let her out. Fortunately, it didn't. That was a sleepless night for us all. We spent many late hours reinforcing the top of the enclosure.

We let Hope and Syra get acquainted through the fence for several days. There was some growling, sniffing and frequent rubbing of noses across the fence line. Hope persistently tried to paw Syra's head. Syra would grumble and growl and hide her face under her huge black furry paws. At feeding time the two would play tug-of-war through the fence with big, juicy bunches of purple grapes—pulling and biting until the grapes flew into the air and bounced like a handful of shiny marbles.

Both bears would run around trying to catch all of the fallen fruit with their quick pink tongues.

As the days passed, the two became more comfortable with each other, so we finally allowed the bears to go into the open area together. For the first few hours, the two cubs went out of their way to ignore each other. By the end of the first day, however, they decided that they'd be friends. Syra walked over to Hope and gave her the slightest lick on her nose. Hope responded by stroking Syra's face gently with her right paw. Since that day, the two have been inseparable. On hot days, you can find them splashing about in their pool; sticking their heads under water, wrestling and playing until they're both soaking wet. Both bears will bound out of the pool and begin a great game of chase all around the enclosure.

By nightfall they are exhausted, and make their way to the wooden shelter to lie draped over each other as they fall into a peaceful sleep.

To this day the two female black bears live contentedly at Wildlife Rescue. Though they will never again know life in the wild, they will always have companionship. Together their years in captivity will be spent side by side, eating, sleeping, swimming and playing together. Life in the wild would have been infinitely better for these two, but life in captivity will be as good as we can make it.

14

The Natural Healer

Several years ago in early June, WRR received a call from one of the San Antonio Fire Departments. In the process of extinguishing an apartment fire, someone had noticed a raccoon trying to escape from the crawl space in the attic. The firefighters had to concentrate on the fire and the human inhabitants of the building, but they wanted to save the raccoon as well. So they called WRR.

When I arrived on the scene, the fire chief on duty met me in the parking lot, immediately took me to a back stairway and escorted me to the attic. There was thick smoke in the building and a portion of the stairs had been scorched, but all in all it was safe, and it was the only way to reach the stranded animal. Once I was there I was able to see that the raccoon had indeed been burned. She was suffering from smoke inhalation as well; she was coughing, confused and having trouble walking. In only a matter of minutes I secured her in a small carrier and was driving her to see one of our veterinarians.

The news from the vet was not good: the young raccoon's feet had been burned, her whiskers were completely singed off, and most of the top layer of her fur was gone. Fortunately, because she was a young animal and would probably tolerate medical treatment in captivity better than an adult wild animal would, her chances for a complete recovery were excellent.

The weeks of treatment began as soon as I set her up in a small holding cage at the Sanctuary. I did not give her very much room because moving around would only aggravate the already tender and fragile condition of her burned paws. The young raccoon was not happy with her new living arrangements. She wanted to climb, to scratch at the door of her cage, to escape, but every time she did so, the pain was so intense that she would stop, sit back, and begin licking her sensitive paws. Every day I applied aloe vera to her wounds. There was no doubt that she was in pain, but I was certain that with the proper care, she would be able to walk again, pain free.

In order to distract her, we placed large bowls of cool water in her cage. At first she would only drink from the bowls, but in a few days she began to place her feet in the cooling water. I was sure that this was providing her some relief from the pain, but as far as the raccoon was concerned, this healing process was taking far too long. She was becoming more and more anxious. Then one day she reminded me of something I had learned years before, but apparently forgotten.

I had an aloe vera plant sitting near her cage, which I was using to help promote her healing. As I opened the door to her cage and began to medicate her burns, the little raccoon reached for the aloe vera plant, snatched off part of the succulent leaves and began to chew them. She swallowed some of them, spit up the others, and rubbed the gooey plant between her two front feet (just as raccoons do when they find a bit of

food in a creek or when they catch a crawfish or small insect). Above all else, this calmed her and obviously made her feel better. As I watched, I remembered the countless stories I had read over the years of how wild animals will find healing herbs and grasses, ingest them, roll in them or do whatever is appropriate, to help them recover from an injury or illness.

From that day forward I gave the fragile young raccoon her very own aloe vera jungle. Each day she gingerly pulled at the leaves, chewed on them, rubbed them between her sore paws, dunked them in her water bowl, drank some of the concoction, played in the leftover puddles, and bit by bit accelerated her own healing.

Finally the day came when I thought she could be moved to an outdoor enclosure. I was a little afraid to move her, because if her wounds were not completely healed the new-found freedom would cause her more discomfort. But I needn't have worried. Once she was out in the bright, warm sunshine, once back in a world that, even though it was fenced, was more like

her real world, the little female raccoon who had been so badly burned suddenly came back to life.

Her first feat was to once again climb a tree. The small oak growing in her enclosure was the perfect place to practice. Each day she passed her tests with flying colors: she could climb, jump and dig with the best of them, and, more importantly, she could do these things just like she used to. After a few months of treatment and confinement, we felt she was ready to return to a normal life. For two more weeks we let her live in the company of two other female raccoons we were preparing for release. Once they all were well acquainted and peacefully interacting, it was time for their big day.

On a warm day in early September, the three raccoon girls were driven to their release site: several hundred acres of privately owned land on the picturesque Guadalupe River that would give them years of food, shelter, trees and other raccoons. The night the cage door was opened, it was no surprise that our former burn victim was the first to come bounding out the door. Some permanent bald areas on her side made her easy to spot. She was also the first one into the trees, and the first one to let me know that once again, given the opportunity, animals will always, with a little help, teach us about patience, perseverance and the ability to heal and once again become whole.

The Scissortail Flycatcher

Every day we take in as many as thirty or forty animals here at the Sanctuary: tiny pink squirrels, slick gray opossum babies, curious furry raccoons crying for their lost mothers. And always seemingly countless numbers of birds.

Birds are often the most challenging of all the patients that we receive: the injured great blue heron, the orphaned green heron, the egg-sized baby night hawks.

The species who feed on the wing—night hawks, chimney swifts, barn swallows and the like—are some of the most difficult to care for without introducing the potentially deadly threat of constant stress. The many species of birds whose primary diet is live insects are also some of the most fragile species when in captivity.

One week we took in an injured adult scissortail flycatcher. The bird had no apparent or severe injuries but he clearly could not fly. At the time the bird was found, there was another adult flycatcher in a nearby oak tree, calling to the

grounded bird. Considering the time of year, there was no question that the bird in the tree was the very concerned mate of the now captive bird.

A closer examination of the bird's wing told us that he was suffering from a dislocated shoulder. This type of injury can be as serious as a broken wing because, even when it is put back in place, the shoulder will sometimes come out again with very little movement.

Another problem is that the time needed for the injury to heal can be as long as two to three weeks. Wild animals are in constant fear when they are suddenly in the company of humans, their number one enemy, which makes them too terrified to eat, much less get well. Fortunately we purchase thousands of live crickets and meal worms specifically for species such as flycatchers, and this bird was one of the more cooperative captive adult flycatchers I've seen. After two days in our nursery, he seemed ready to be moved to a larger outside cage. All we could do was place the scissortail there and hope he would continue to eat so that we would not have to force-feed him.

After a close watch for twenty-four hours, and a dozen crickets and meal worms later, we were relieved to see that the injured bird was indeed going to eat on his own. Now there was nothing left to do but give him plenty of peace, quiet, privacy and live food, and hope his shoulder would mend.

A week went by and the bird was still doing well. He had adjusted somewhat to his temporary life in captivity. He was eating his fill of insects and his shoulder was not quite as tender as when he first came in. There was a real chance that this bird would survive and be able to be returned to his home, and perhaps his mate. After the second week, the scissortail was looking great. He was strong and active and we felt sure he was ready to go back home.

I had little hope that after two weeks his mate would still be waiting, but I knew that if they had a nest of young, she would be caring for them and would therefore still be in the area.

The day finally came for the long-awaited release. Staff member Tim Ajax took the flycatcher back to the site where he had been found, an open field with two huge oak trees that dotted the fence line.

The carrying cage holding the once-crippled bird was opened and he looked out onto the field. No doubt the sight of home was all he needed to fly free of his crate.

He went straight up into the air and as he did he called out in the unmistakable scissortail "kew-kew." The shrill call immediately alerted the very patient mate, who was awaiting in the nearby oak. She called repeatedly to the now free bird, no doubt asking where he had been and letting him know she was glad to have him back. The two birds lingered in the tall oak trees, back together, healthy and ready to continue their life as a family.

WRR takes in almost 2000 birds every year. Though the majority of these are released, it is not often that the birds we rescue are actually reunited with their families back in their original home. For us here at the Sanctuary, this was one of those perfect endings to all our hard work.

16

Snapshots from the Sanctuary

Orphan baby raccoon whose mother had been shot.

A rescued javelina.

Hybrid wolf rescued from a roadside zoo.

Indian Runner ducks, unwanted pets rescued by WRR.

Injured Muscovy in a medicated bath.

Mountain lions
confiscated from
private "owners"
because of abuse.

Capuchin monkey confiscated at Mexican border.

Elderly female Capuchin rescued from cruel confinement in a basement.

Spider monkey
discarded by
"owner."

Spider monkey rescued
along with fifty other
monkeys from the
basement of a home.

Jaguar rescued after
a severe beating.

Hybrid fox rescued from fur "farm" where he was being bred for pelts.

Orphan baby skunks who are being rehabilitated to be released.

Thanksgiving turkeys rescued from a slaughterhouse.

Free-roaming black vulture who lives
at the Sanctuary.

Juvenile screech owl being rehabilitated for release.

"Hybrid wolf" rescued from exploitation in the pet trade.

Orphan baby bobcat rescued
after her mother was killed
by a car.

17

The Baby Field Mouse

One day, Pinhead, one of my many cats, brought me a small and quite terrified baby field mouse. Fortunately, Pinhead hadn't harmed the mouse, she only held him in her mouth for a time. I searched the fields around my house to try to find the baby's nest, but wasn't successful. I decided the best thing to do was to try to raise him until he was old enough to be set free. This wasn't going to be easy. His mouth was so minute I could barely find it, and it would be difficult to feed him enough to keep him alive. I decided this baby needed a momma mouse, so I went to a pet shop and rescued one, along with her family of babies. I took the family home and introduced the field mouse to his new mom and siblings. It was instant acceptance. The momma mouse began licking and cleaning her new baby, and the other young mice seemed not to mind having a new wild brother. Everything was going well, I thought.

Early the following morning, when I checked on the mouse family, I was shocked to find the momma mouse dead. She

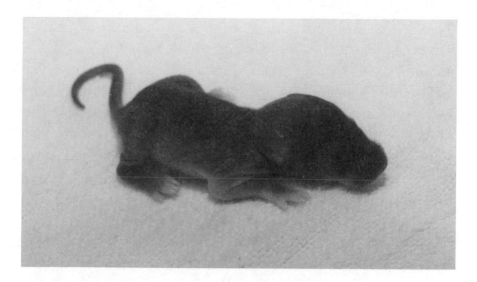

had appeared to be perfectly healthy. It was as if she had simply gone to sleep and did not wake up. I removed her from the box and buried her in the field. Now, I was faced with raising not just one orphan mouse but fourteen. All of my syringes were too large to feed any of these mice. Some still had their eyes shut and they were all tiny. With the help of veterinarian Dr. Robert Granberry, I devised a feeding implement—a long plastic needle cover attached to a tuberculin syringe. I bought a week's supply of Esbilac—an orphan puppy formula—and set about the task of feeding some of the smallest orphans I've ever worked with. Fortunately, all of the mice were very hungry, which made them very cooperative. Each time I held the feeding tube to their mouths, they'd stick out their tiny pink tongues and lap up the entire syringe of formula. Because they were so young, they could tolerate only small amounts of formula each feeding. This meant that they would need to be fed at least twice every hour.

As the weeks passed, I was amazed as I watched the baby mice continue to grow and eat and develop into juvenile mice.

They were slowly but surely beginning to take care of themselves. All fourteen were learning to chew on Johnson grass, as well as whole wheat bread, nuts and dried fruit. They even began burrowing into the fresh hay in their box. Finally they were becoming self-sufficient with little or no need for formula, feeding tubes or my constant care. There is always a sense of relief when baby animals outgrow their need of intensive, day-to-day care. For these little guys, I was just happy they had survived.

Soon it was time to set the field mouse free. I set up a release box just for him, full of hay, fresh seed, bread, fruit and a jar lid of water. I cut a small hole in one side and faced it to a dense woodpile in the field. He would now have the choice of leaving the security of the box entirely, or coming and going while he made the adjustment of returning to his environment.

On his first night out in his box, the little mouse ventured into the woodpile. He seemed curious but cautious about his new surroundings. Little by little, he investigated the woodpile and the grassy area around it. After the third day, he seemed comfortable with his surroundings and abandoned the box for his life in the wild.

I'm sure he's living with wild field mice now, but I'm just as sure he'll remember his days with his family of domestic mice. The other thirteen are quite content to live in their permanent home, a large cage with sleeping boxes, potted plants and their very own bale of hay. It sits out in the same field where the field mouse lives. Perhaps he even comes around and visits his adopted family. And just maybe, he and Pinhead exchange friendly glances when their paths cross.

18

The Female Bobcat

When I started WRR my primary goal was to save the lives of as many wild animals as possible. I always knew I was willing to do whatever it took to accomplish that goal. I am happy and satisfied to be able to say that the number of those animals whose lives we have saved is indeed too many to count.

One of the most memorable of these was a two-year-old female bobcat who had spent most of her days in a small closet. WRR was asked to remove her from the city limits. Her "owners" had grown tired of her, and predictably, she had grown quite wild in her behavior. To control her, they had locked her in a bedroom closet. When I learned of the deplorable condition in which the bobcat was being held, I knew it was vital to get to her as soon as I could.

It was early on a Sunday morning when I arrived at my destination. A young man met me at the door. I was escorted down a narrow hallway to a small bedroom at the back of the house. I remember vividly walking over to the old, wooden door that shut the captive cat away from the rest of the world.

It was warped and difficult to open. As I pulled on the old glass door knob I could hear the low rumbling. The cat inside was as frightened as she was angry, all she wanted to do was get out of her "cage." When I offered her a large crate to run into she took me up on my offer—no questions asked.

Wildlife Rescue was able to provide the cat with her own spacious, grassy enclosure. I took her to the Sanctuary and watched as she cautiously crept out of her crate and into her new home.

I don't believe I have ever seen such a look of relief as I saw in that beautiful bobcat's eyes that day. I remember feeling so pleased that WRR could give her a better home than she had known in her short life. I also remember assuming that she would have to live the rest of her life in captivity, since she had never lived in the wild. It wasn't long before she began to teach me a very valuable lesson about wild animals.

After only a few weeks I began seeing signs that this cat was capable of hunting as she began to behave more and more like a wild animal every day. Thankfully she had not been declawed, like so many bobcats that come to us. I started to realize that this bobcat could—with a little help—be set free to live the way she should have lived from the beginning.

I spent the following few months preparing the cat for her big day, as well as picking out the right place for her release. After contacting several of our members whose properties were used as protected release sites, I finally found the perfect place, a ranch in South Texas, miles from

any houses, with large stock tanks, that also had a healthy bobcat population. To be sure we could track this cat after she was set free, the veterinarian shaved some small patches of her fur during her final check-up. This was the least intrusive way of identifying her so we could be sure she remained healthy in the wild. Because she was released on privately-owned property, the landowners would be able to watch out for her. We set up a feeding station so she could find food if she had trouble hunting, this also served as an observation site.

When the time came to release the bobcat she was taken to the selected site and set up in a temporary cage where she would spend her first two nights, giving her time to get ac-

quainted with the new area. On the third day, we set her free. I had some doubts about her ability to survive, but I felt certain that if she encountered any problems we would be able to set a live trap to catch her so we could reevaluate her situation. Several days passed before she was seen again, but it was a big relief to learn that

she was not particularly interested in her supplemental food. This of course indicated that she was most likely hunting on her own and required no additional help. As the months passed the bobcat was frequently seen on the property. She always appeared to be healthy and doing well in her new natural life. Although there were always other WRR challenges that needed tending to and other animals to care for, part of my heart and thoughts were with that bobcat in the wild.

Then, well into the summer, I received a report from the ranch. Although our bobcat still appeared healthy and well-fed, her behavior had changed noticeably. She seemed more cautious, even nervous. When the landowners investigated, they found that our female bobcat, who had been rescued from the darkness of a tiny closet, had now become the proud mother of two beautiful kittens!

Born naturally in the wild, the playful and curious kittens never strayed far from their mother's side. As soon as Mother

Bobcat realized she was being watched, she took her family back into the safety of the dense underbrush. It was then that I finally knew there was no question that this beautiful, intelligent cat had learned not only how to survive, but indeed to thrive, in her natural habitat.

19

The Great Horned Owl

Throughout the year, we take in and care for thousands of wild animals. Many spend several months in our care; others need our attention for a year or more. Every so often, we're happy to take in one of those rare creatures who needs us for only a few days.

Such was a case of one very thin, battered and worn-out great horned owl. The call came in from a woman who had noticed a large bird sitting at the bottom of a telephone pole. He had been there for quite some time, maybe a day or two. She said that his left eye was swollen shut and appeared to have a wire sticking out of it. The bird allowed her to pick him up. Since he made no attempt to fly away, she knew he was in real trouble. She placed him in a large bird cage and called Wildlife Rescue.

When we arrived at the woman's home, she took us to a side yard. There in the cage sat an adult great horned owl, barely able to hold up his head. His left eye was severely infected. Upon closer examination, I noticed that what appeared to be wires were actually feathers around the eye that were so encrusted from the infection they had become hard and dry, preventing the eye from opening. As I peeled each tiny, dry feather away, I could see that the injury was several days old. In fact, I wasn't at all sure that he still had an eye.

The owl was so debilitated that he did not even struggle as I worked to open his eyelid. He just sat patiently, watching my every move with his one good eye. His large beak would open slowly to warn me that he was not totally incapacitated. I noticed that his beak was chipped and scarred, and felt certain that—if he could talk—he would have many stories to tell about how he acquired all his battle scars.

He was bone thin and would need immediate care if he was to recover fully. That evening, I cleaned and medicated his injured eye and fed him small strips of beef heart soaked in water. He would take these from my hand reluctantly, but he was anything but shy when it came to devouring half a cup of food from a dish.

By the next morning, it was obvious that the old owl was feeling a little better. He wasn't as cooperative about taking his medication, but he was very interested in breakfast. He ate two pulverized chicken necks and a large portion of beef heart.

Day two arrived and the first thing I saw when I checked on the owl were two large gold eyes staring back at me. Though the injured eye was cloudy, it was wide open and blinking. This bird, once weak and timid, was now standing straight, perched on a large branch in his cage. And he was definitely not interested in being hand-fed. He was even less enthusiastic about being medicated, but we compromised. As long as I let him feed himself, he would tolerate my medicating his eye.

By the fifth day, the great horned owl was eating every bit of food and demanding second helpings. His eye was still a bit cloudy and he moved cautiously about his cage, indicating that his vision was still poor.

After three more days of medication, the owl's injured eye was as clear and bright as his good eye. He was beginning to refuse the extra portions of food, eating only what a healthy owl would normally eat.

On the tenth day, the owl would no longer tolerate my care. He was well again and all he wanted was his freedom. I waited until dusk to open his cage door. I knew the Sanctuary was the best place to release him because he had been found only about three miles away. If he had a mate waiting for him, he would surely find his way back.

It took about three seconds for the great horned owl to notice that his cage door had been left open. He released the perch from the grip of his huge talons, and as he approached the open door, he spread his broad wings. Two steps and he was through the door and into the field. He stood there for a few minutes, looking about, getting his bearings. He hopped several feet towards a tall hackberry tree. Then, with the silent flapping of his great wings, he flew up to the tree. He gazed out towards the east, ruffled his feathers and took to the evening sky. His flight was perfect. As I watched him soar high above the tall oak trees, I was relieved to see that he could maintain his altitude. Then, in flawless, quiet flight, the old great horned owl disappeared into the horizon, back safe and free again in his world.

The Macaque Sisters

Some of the most rewarding rescues over the years have been those in which we have taken animals from a living hell and brought them into a life of peace and safety. I once received a call from a woman in Washington who had heard about two crab-eating macaques who were going to be retired from eighteen years of work in a research facility. The monkeys were sisters and had been taken from the wild when they were still babies.

These two brave sisters had long ago been deprived of a life of sunshine and cool breezes. After being captured in the late 1970s, their lives consisted of constant confinement and a day-in day-out life sentence dictated by human need and curiosity. We will never know what life is like for a wild and free-roaming animal who suddenly finds herself in captivity. I can only imagine that the adjustment must be profoundly difficult. To go from tree climbing, food gathering and interacting with various family members to a life of sterility and isolation must surely be a living hell. When I learned that we had the opportunity to give these two monkeys a new life, I knew we could not say no.

Quickly we had to go about the task of building an enclosure next to the rhesus macaque, and her friend, the little female crab-eating macaque from Florida. With a tall oak tree and several bushy cedars, it was the perfect home for the two new monkeys.

After weeks of labor on the part of our staff, the day finally came for the eighteen-year-old sisters to arrive. They were being driven in from Washington by their rescuers. The day was sunny and warm. The monkeys sat quietly in the transport cages as we carried them to their new home. Their eyes were wide and bright as they surveyed the Sanctuary. Chickens strutted about and a beautiful blue peacock displayed his plumage. The rhesus monkey came to see who her new neighbors were and the crab-eating macques were looking on to see what all the excitement was about.

As their wire carrying cage touched the ground, the monkeys' soft, naked feet felt the gentle earth for the first time in many years. Their eyes darted from side to side as I immediately opened their door to freedom. Finally, the two monkeys had come home. As the shy sisters peered through the door, one bolted out and leaped fearlessly into the limbs of the oak tree hanging overhead. The other could not wait any longer. She sprang up into the tree and met her sister on a large, leafy branch.

The sisters' eyes met as they sat together in a tree for the first time in eighteen years. Their hands touched as they watched the world around them come to life. There were clouds racing past the warm sun and small brown sparrows perched near them in their tree. Strangely, there were no stainless steel cages, no walls and no foreign odors. Just fresh air, green leaves and that huge, warm sun. How long, in  their memories, had it been since Nature wrapped her warm, loving arms around them? How could they have lived so long deprived of that birthright?

As the two sisters began investigating every tiny bit of the huge oak tree, they noticed that they were being watched. The female rhesus and crab-eating macaque were staring at their new neighbors. The crab-eating macaque sensed something very familiar about these two new monkeys. They were just like her. Without hesitation, all three crab-eating macaques began smacking their lips and gently grabbing at each other's hair in an attempt to groom one another through the fence. As the day progressed, the two monkeys became more overwhelmed with their new surroundings. I wondered how they would feel as the sun began to set and they would spend their first night out of doors.

I watched their enclosure as darkness fell. Neither of the sisters could sleep. They looked at the chickens going one by one to roost in a nearby tree. They looked curiously in another direction as the first great horned owl began to hoot. The moon slowly rose up into the night sky and they sat close together and drank in the view. For an entire day and into the night, these two brave sisters saw what to them was a whole new world. But not so new that the memories of their past were not stirred . . . those long-ago memories of days spent playfully in the treetops, those ancient memories that now have finally come home to them.

21

The Fawn
and the Doe

One day a very frightened female white-tail deer soared through a plate glass window at a northside realty office. In doing so, the terrified animal ripped open her stomach on the jagged glass. Fortunately, the employees contacted WRR immediately and a volunteer rushed to the aid of the injured doe. It was apparent upon her arrival that the deer needed emergency medical treatment, so with the help of the Parks and Wildlife Department game warden, the doe was taken to the nearby animal hospital. There the veterinarian sedated her and, after a quick examination, discovered that she was about to give birth.

There was little hope that the baby would survive the Caesarean delivery because in most cases either the fawn or the mother dies, and in many cases, neither of the animals survives the trauma. But we all believe in miracles here at WRR so we said a little prayer and kept our fingers crossed. Once the tiny fawn was safely removed from her mother's torn womb,

she just lay there, wet and fragile and helpless. It seemed like hours, but in only a few seconds the little miracle began to breathe. We were relieved to see that there was a chance she would survive, but there was still a tremendous amount of work to be done. We had a new baby to feed and a mother who had to be taken immediately to the Sanctuary to recover from the surgery and anesthesia.

We rushed the two critical animals to their next phase of treatment. Once at the Sanctuary the tiny female fawn was slowly bottle-fed warm fawn formula (her mother could no longer nurse her because of her own wounds and the stitches from her surgery); she was kept on a heating pad so that she could stabilize her body temperature. It was touch-and-go with the baby because she had absorbed some of the drugs given to her mother during the surgery. We had to be sure she could swallow and that she did not aspirate any of the formula. We also had to consider the danger she was in from not having any of the natural immunities she would have received from her mother's milk. Fortunately, we keep colostrum on hand at the Sanctuary for just these kinds of emergencies.

Once we had the fawn warm and her tummy full, it was time to begin stabilizing her mother, who was just beginning to wake up. Deer are nervous animals and this poor doe had just been through what was certainly one of the worst days of her life. Now, she was about to discover herself in totally unfamiliar surroundings. As she tried to shake off the anesthetic she wobbled, her head fell to the side, and her tongue draped lifelessly from her mouth, making her look all the more pathetic and helpless. Fortunately, she was smart enough to realize she could not stand up, and took advantage of our soft bed of hay and blankets. All we could do was watch and hope.

Several hours passed and little by little the doe regained her strength. Now every time we approached her enclosure, she would run frantically into the side fence, so we had to keep our distance while still attempting to keep a close eye on her. As the day ended it was easy to see that she was going to fully recover from the drugs. She was now able to pull her tongue back into her mouth and she could drink water, even though she was not yet steady on her feet. We knew the next day would tell us just how fully she was going to recover.

The following morning the new fawn was stronger and more alert. She was almost able to maintain her body temperature and she was fully capable of nursing from a bottle. The doe, however, was not looking as well as we had hoped. She was awake and on her feet, but she showed no interest in eating

and was beginning to show the classic signs of depression that one often sees in adult wild animals who suddenly realize they are unable to go free. Because the vet had used sutures that did not have to be removed and given the doe a long-acting antibiotic, we knew we could set her free any time we felt she was able to go. Now came the hard part—making the decision of whether to release Mom without ever letting her see her baby, or holding on to her in hopes that somehow they could spend some time together, even though she would not be able to feed her fawn.

There is something so tragic about separating a baby from her mother. But we have to look far beyond our own feelings and consider only what is best for the animals. Every time we approached the doe she exhibited nothing but fear, running headlong into the fence and darting blindly around the enclosure. She did not seem to realize that the fawn was her baby, and since there had been absolutely no contact between the two because the doe was completely sedated when the fawn was taken from her, there was no way to know if she would know her fawn. By that evening, it was clear that there was only one action we could take that would continue to ensure the survival of both mother and baby. We had to set the mother free.

The sun was just about to set, the day had cooled down and all was quiet at the Sanctuary. We slowly opened the gate to the doe's enclosure. She still had no reason to trust any of us, so we backed off to let her take her time deciding what to do. As the sky grew darker the doe felt more secure. This was her time of day, and she could now see her way to freedom. All she had to do was stride through that gate and be on her way. She approached the opening quietly and gracefully. She knew we were near but somehow she also knew that now she had a choice. She took one slow step through the open gate and peered out at the trees and tall grass leading away from the enclosure. She took three more slow steps that took her down the rocky ledge toward the back of the Sanctuary. Now she could finally relax. She perked up her ears and listened for every hint of sound that might tell her of danger or safety, and then proceeded down the ledge to the open field surrounded only by more dense trees and tall grasses. She strode past the coyote enclosure looking now quite fearless, perhaps realizing that the coyotes were captive and she was not. Though the coyotes howled, there was no fear in her beautiful brown eyes.

It was sad to see her go, but it was encouraging to realize that the result of all our hard work was a healthy adult doe who had somehow beat all odds and proved again that you can believe in miracles.

Now we have one more little orphan fawn to care for who is nothing short of a miracle herself. And even though she has lost her mother, she has the companionship of over sixty-five other orphan fawns, and one day she too, will be set free—just like Mom.

Bertha, Huey and the Bachelor Duck

Wildlife Rescue has, for years, come to the aid of count-less domestic ducks and geese. Back in the seventies when it was more commonplace to see fluffy yellow babies being sold as Easter "pets," it was also commonplace for WRR to be called on to rescue these babies once the novelty of watching them swim in the bathtub wore off. Ducks and geese are remark-able animals. I have always found them to be intelligent, play-ful, gregarious and quite willing to be spoiled by any human who is fortunate enough to find herself in their company. Over the years I have watched adult geese come here to the Sanc-tuary after spending years in tiny cages, in backyards, con-fined in cement slab dog runs, or nearly starved to death in crates in flea markets and pet shops.

Several year ago I had the distinct privilege of meeting two very special domestic geese named Bertha and Huey. Huey was named after the cartoon goose, Baby Huey. The cartoon Baby Huey would waddle about, his rather rotund body

sparsely covered by a dia-
per that didn't quite fit,
eating tons of food. He
probably wasn't all that
bright, unlike the Huey I
know who was as intelli-
gent as any goose I ever
met.

Bertha and Huey came
from very humble begin-
nings. WRR received a call
from a young girl who had
gone into a feed store to
purchase some food for
her duck and was very upset to see two beautiful geese stuffed
into a wire cage. Upon close examination she discovered that
Bertha's feet were being eaten by the collection of maggots
gathered in the filth that had not been cleaned from the bottom of the cage. Huey was doing his best to comfort Bertha:
he kept grooming her neck and her back, and continually
nudged her to keep moving about the cage floor so the maggots would not have the advantage of an immobile target.

As soon as I arrived at the feed store I could see that I
didn't have any time to waste. Both of the geese were thin and
they appeared to be severely dehydrated. There was no water
in their cage and the small food bowl was dusty on the bottom. There was no way of knowing how long it had been since
these two brave birds had eaten a decent meal and enjoyed a
drink of clean water. After a brief and unpleasant chat with
the owner of the feed store, I paid the ten dollar asking price
(five dollars per goose), gathered my new charges and drove
straight to the Sanctuary.

The first few days at their new home, Bertha and Huey did little more than eat and drink. In their new surroundings of soft grass and their very own wading pool, Bertha was able to walk about pain-free. Each day Huey would sit close by as we soaked Bertha's dried and hole-ridden feet in vitamin E oil. After her therapy Bertha would waddle over to Huey's side, nuzzle her beak into his soft neck feathers and there in the tall Bermuda grass they would take their afternoon nap together.

As the weeks went on, Bertha and Huey made friends with several of the other geese and ducks living at the Sanctuary. They would honk and quack and waddle about, Bertha never quite able to keep up, Huey always waiting for her as the other birds made their way down to the pond and into the cool water for a morning swim. Little by little Bertha and Huey realized that finally they had a new home where they were safe and comfortable—so comfortable that they decided to raise a family.

Bertha was the first of the two geese to set up housekeeping. She could be seen walking around the Sanctuary grounds picking out just the right twigs and leaves and clumps of grass. She decided the best nest site would be their favorite grassy spot right next to their wading pool. Once her nest was constructed, Bertha gently pulled out several of her own downy feathers, making the top layer of the nest soft and warm for the soon-to-be-laid eggs. As Bertha settled onto her nest and laid one big, cream-colored egg, Huey could sense that she was not going to budge. He wasn't exactly sure what was going on. He would go off for a swim and there Bertha would sit, not willing to leave her egg to grow cold without her.

Not far from Bertha and Huey's nest sat a friend of theirs, a bachelor Muscovy duck. This beautiful dark green and white male had never really found his true love and for some reason he seemed to prefer the company of Bertha and Huey over that of his duck companions. The bachelor duck watched patiently as Bertha sat on her egg. On occasion he would waddle down to the pond with Huey, but as always he would return to sit near the nest site just watching and, I imagine, waiting for the big day when that egg would hatch. Little did I know that the bachelor duck had even more in mind.

One very hot afternoon Bertha grew tired of sitting on her family-to-be. Huey was trying his very best to coax her off the nest and down to the pond to swim with him and the other geese. He would honk and honk and waddle impatiently back and forth in front of Bertha as if to say "Come on, that egg can live without you for a few minutes!" Bertha would squirm about restlessly on the nest, wanting to leave, but not being sure if she should. Not, that is, until a friend came to her aid.

On this hot afternoon as Huey coaxed and Bertha tried to decide what to do, the bachelor duck made his way to the nest. The more Bertha squirmed, the closer he moved to the egg. Finally Bertha stood up and took two short steps towards Huey, and as she did, the bachelor duck gently moved in under her and placed his body on top of that big, cream-colored goose egg. He did not quite cover the nest, but there he sat, perched atop that huge pile of sticks and grass. Bertha turned, looked at her new babysitter, pecked him once on the top of his head and slowly waddled down to the pond with her mate. As Bertha and Huey swam, the bachelor duck sat on "his" egg.

When the geese returned, bachelor duck relinquished his post and once again took up his place nearby waiting for the next time Bertha would need a babysitter. The Muscovy duck didn't have long to wait. The very next day, in the afternoon, Huey called on Bertha and down to the pond they went. In fact, every afternoon the two geese would go for their swim while their bachelor friend took over the duties of nestsitting.

When the big day finally came, the one big egg hatched, Bertha sat, the proud new mother goose, beside Huey and Bachelor Duck, the two proud new fathers. The day that the new baby goose followed Bertha and Huey to the pond for his first swim, there at the back of the line, watching over "his baby" was Bachelor Duck. Even though he never found a mate, he always had a family in Bertha and Huey, the two rescued geese.

The Crippled Raccoon

Every time I see a raccoon suffering from any illness, I remember a unique baby raccoon who came to Wildlife Rescue several years ago. The call came that spring morning from a construction site where the workers had seen the youngster in the area for a couple of days. Eventually, they caught the little animal and put him in a huge, deep garbage bin. We were then called on to rescue him.

When he first came in, the young male had little use of his back legs. He was thin and dehydrated and could barely walk. But he did have a good appetite. Big bowls full of fresh, juicy grapes, slices of banana, and kitten chow were some of his favorites.

The juvenile coon would cry and fuss if he had to spend too much time in his cage, but it was difficult to leave him in the company of other raccoons, due to his inability to walk. The other raccoons would climb all over him. The best we could do for him, to be sure he had exercise, was to let him

110

"run" around the Sanctuary house. The little guy took great joy in doing this. He seemed to focus all of his concentration on trying to regain the use of his back legs. He tried to stand. He tried to climb up onto everything that was well above floor level. He tried to run and play. The small recovering raccoon crawled his way into everyone's heart.

One day, as the raccoon was making his way around the kitchen floor, one of the staff members dropped several TUMS®, which the coon immediately ate. Whatever the reason, the little raccoon made a point of adding TUMS® to his daily diet.

He had such a will to live—to grow and become a "complete" raccoon. He would frequently overturn bowls of water and spend hours playing in the mess. As his appetite increased, so did his size and weight. Because his prognosis was not good, and I knew that a fat, crippled raccoon would not have an easy life, I decided it was time to put the little guy on a diet.

As the weeks passed, the coon grew in size and strength. He was able to pull his legs up under him and stand for several minutes at a time. He was becoming too wild and too big to continue living in the house. It was time for him to learn to live outside and learn how to be a "real" raccoon.

We placed him in a large outdoor enclosure with three other raccoons his same age. There were large tree limbs to climb and sturdy wooden boxes for sleeping. There was a deep, soft bed of hay and a small pool of water. The three raccoons soon became the best of friends. They spent their days sleeping and their nights climbing about in the tree branches.

As I watched them over the weeks, it was easy to see that our coon with the sweet tooth for TUMS® was progressing far beyond our most optimistic hopes. Though his back legs were not perfect in their skills of climbing and running, they were able to let the half-grown male keep up with his roommates. It seemed that the more space he had, the more he lived up to the challenge.

By early autumn, it was clear that the raccoon and his buddies were ready to return to a life in the wild. It was difficult for me to let him go, knowing that he was not completely recovered. He, I am sure, never gave his "condition" a second thought.

One night, before we had decided on a specific release date, our group of raccoons decided to set *themselves* free. There was a metal latch on the door to their enclosure, which they seemed to know was the only thing keeping them from the river, the tall oak and cypress trees, the green pastures and . . . freedom. The raccoons worked the latch loose and made their exit. By morning they were nowhere to be found. I left a big bowl of food out for the escapees and, as expected, they were back the next evening ready for dinner.

For several months after their release, the coon buddies stayed in the area. Every night they returned for their meal and every night the once immobile raccoon was right there with them: climbing, running, and of course, eating. He had finally made his way back to his world.

24

The Two Bobcats

When I founded Wildlife Rescue, I had business cards printed with my home telephone number and distributed them to individuals and agencies that might come in contact with animals in need of help. One of the first calls I received concerned a young bobcat. She had been found sitting in a small aquarium in a pet shop, and seemed to be bleeding to death after being brutally declawed. A family had gone to the pet shop, saw the terrified cat and decided to rescue her. The only problem was that once they had her at home and spent several days treating her wounds, feeding her and trying to calm her down, they weren't sure what to do next. They decided to call us.

Wildlife Rescue at that time was basically one person in one small house in San Antonio. I did have a veterinarian who helped out as a volunteer whenever he could. I knew I had to take that bobcat in and do whatever I could for her. She was quite wild and not interested in becoming tame. I turned over two rooms in my house to her. Here she could at least climb bookcases, sleep on furniture and gaze out the windows watching for birds and squirrels. Not the perfect life by any means, but better than a pet shop aquarium.

Weeks went by and she kept to herself. She'd come down off her bookcase to eat. I set up some big tree limbs for her to climb and, on occasion, she'd use those. But all in all, she wanted nothing to do with me. I didn't force the issue. After all, she was wild.

Then, early one morning, the perfect solution found its way to my front door. A large wooden crate had been left on the porch with this note attached: "Please find me a good home. I can no longer live with my human family. I have nowhere else to go. All I have with me is my red sock."

I peered into the darkened crate, at first expecting to find a puppy, but all that purring was not coming from an abandoned puppy. A rather large cat, I thought, must go with those big round yellow eyes. I took the crate into my living room and under the watchful eye of the declawed bobcat kitten, I began to break into the sealed door. The abandoned "pet" was none other than a young, declawed male bobcat. The difference between him and the female was that this fellow thought people were the neatest thing since sliced bread. All he was interested in was rubbing up against my legs and pretending to sharpen his claws on my furniture. This went on for about twenty minutes. He purred and rubbed, never noticing that we had company.

Suddenly, after he decided he was comfortable with his new home, the young cat began to sniff around his new surroundings. All his attention was quickly focused at the upper right-hand corner of the tall wooden bookcase. It was there that their eyes first met. His, full of curiosity and playfulness. Hers, full of challenge and fear.

She had no intention of letting this playful newcomer share her home. All he wanted was to make friends and get on with the business of playing chase or catch or anything else he could get away with. Days passed. Weeks passed. She remained distant and aloof. He remained hopeful and optimistic. At least they were peacefully sharing their area of the house with no fights, lots of tolerance, separate food bowls, separate water bowls and their own corners for sleeping.

I could only assume that the clever young male was scheming every minute of every day to come up with the perfect plan to win over his reluctant roommate.

Late one night, when the house was quiet, I decided to sit and watch the two bobcats to see if they were making any progress. The male was making his usual rounds, walking over to the first shelf of the bookcase, looking up at the silent female, unyielding from her perch on the top shelf. When he would make advances toward the second shelf, she would begin to growl. He would back away, pacing around the room, considering his next move.

All at once, struck by inspiration, he darted into his crate, grabbed his red sock, ran to the bottom of the bookcase and lay there on his back, fondling and grabbing his favorite toy. He took that bright red sock and pulled on it with his teeth, dangled it between his paws, and tossed it up in the air. He was a kitten all over again.

The female, for the first time, actually looked down from her perch with interest and curiosity. She was still such a young cat that playtime was perhaps something she wasn't quite ready to give up.

The male paid her no attention. He was having a great time on his own, throwing his sock, drooling on it, running across the hardwood floor and bringing it back to his spot at the foot of the bookcase. Nothing was going to stop him from having a good time. Not even one very timid female bobcat who was

slowly making her way down the bookcase onto the tree limb. She sat for over half an hour, watching. He looked up once in a while, just to let her know that he saw her. Finally, after an hour or more had passed, she made her move, slinking slowly toward the red sock lying beside the now-exhausted male. She stretched out her battered little paw and gently took the prized sock as her own. The agreeable male simply watched, doing nothing to stop or discourage her. She began to sniff the sock and bat it about on the floor. He lay still, letting her play.

In the hours that followed, it became obvious that the young male had won the fe-male over by doing nothing, just letting her do whatever she was comfortable with.

After that, the two cats became inseparable. They ate together, slept together and played together. They lived in Wildlife Rescue's care for over thirteen years, first at our old Sanctuary and then at our current location.

In the summer of 1991, they died within weeks of each other, first the female and then the male. It is impossible to say what life would have been for these two cats had Wildlife Rescue not been there. As it was, in the place of freedom, the only gift they had was each other's constant companionship.

Miles and Priscilla

It was just days before Thanksgiving one year when a young man was driving behind a huge tractor-trailer truck filled to capacity with beautiful white turkeys, no doubt making their final journey. As the truck approached a bridge, it slowed, swerved and finally tipped over completely, crashing on its side. The truck lay there motionless. Frightened turkeys were calling from inside their tiny wire boxes. Suddenly, several of the doors sprang open. In a flash, turkeys were fleeing in all directions.

The truck driver, apparently unharmed, started running around trying to capture the liberated birds. After about fifteen minutes, he threw his hands in the air and gave up the fight.

Our turkey rescuer was watching this drama unfold from only yards away. He waited for the perfect opportunity. Soon the driver was busy checking on the birds still confined in their cages. Quietly, the young man walked toward the area

where he had last seen the emancipated turkeys. There, in a grassy pasture, he spotted a group of four birds. Two were pecking curiously in the deep grass. The other two were nestled quietly in a thick patch of weeds. He later described them as looking as though "they were waiting for the end to come."

As he approached the big white birds, two turkeys ran away into the fields that would now be their new home. The two more reluctant birds sat very still and frightened. Little did they know that the individual who would usher them into their new life was standing before them.

When the turkey couple arrived at the Sanctuary, it was easy to see that they were inseparable. As the pair emerged from their giant cardboard box, they didn't run or try to find the nearest bush to hide under. Instead, they took quick, deliberate steps out of their past, where they had faced certain and imminent death, into the security of their new home.

Immediately, they were surrounded by peacocks, ducks, geese and chickens. There were huge bowls full to the brim with fresh corn and millet. There were wading pools overflowing with clean, cool water. There were giant oak trees filled with chirping, perching birds, free to fly about as they wished. These were not familiar sights in their former environment. There had been no place to take a relaxing and enjoyable dust bath. But here at the Sanctuary, the turkeys found all these luxuries and more. Here was an atmosphere of safety. The air didn't smell of fear or death. Like the turkeys, other domestic

birds went about their day, eating and strutting. And, most importantly, living.

Although we never name the wild animals living at the Sanctuary which we plan on releasing, in honor of Thanksgiving Day, the volunteers named the two domestic turkeys Miles and Priscilla. The couple lived peacefully at the Sanctuary for six years. Each day, they'd walk about the grounds, finding insects, feasting on scratch feed and juicy chunks of apple and pear. They lived their lives in the company of one another and when the time came, they died together.

Early one autumn morning as I was making my rounds, I noticed Miles sitting alone under a huge Juniper tree. Nearby was a large pile of newly-fallen soft brown leaves. In the center lay Priscilla. She had died in her sleep the night before, but Miles would not leave her side. At noon, he was still sitting next to her. Though I couldn't leave her body there for long, I also could not bear to take her from him. I decided to leave the two together overnight. It turned out to be the best thing. When I found Miles the next morning, he was right next to her. He too had died in his sleep, never once leaving her side.

26

The Squirrel Determined to be a Mama

Late one Friday afternoon, a young man driving down East Mulberry in San Antonio watched in shock as the car in front of him hit a squirrel trying to cross the street. The car didn't stop, but the young man, wanting to help the injured animal, screeched to a halt, jumped out of his car, stopped oncoming traffic and gently scooped up the seemingly lifeless little body. As he carried the squirrel to his car, he could only think of how to dispose of the now-deceased animal. He placed her in the back seat and drove home.

When he pulled into his driveway, he remembered an old cardboard box he had in his garage. As he opened the back door of his car, there sat the injured squirrel, shaky, not quite able to use her back legs, but very much alive. The young man placed the box over her and ran into the house to call his vet. By now, it was well after six in the evening and no clinics were open. One vet, however, gave him our phone number. We told him to bring the squirrel to the Sanctuary. When our hero arrived, he was relieved to have finally found help for the animal.

The next thing to do was stabilize the injured squirrel, assess her wounds and hope that she wasn't suffering from a broken back or internal bleeding. Within an hour, it was apparent that this was one fortunate creature. Her fragile hind legs had been badly scraped and bruised, several small patches of fur were missing and she had a slight tilt to her head, indicating some degree of head or spinal trauma. Somehow this small, wild animal had survived a major collision with a metal object fifty times her size. I had every hope that, with our care and plenty of time to rest and regain her strength, this young female squirrel could be returned to her life of freedom.

Several days passed. Our new patient was still not able to pick up her food, so we were force-feeding her several times a day. She was terrified every time we came near her cage, but for now, it was the only way. Finally, she began using her front paws to scoop up the small pieces of pecans, apples and pears to her mouth. Then she'd lift each piece with her tongue, take a few bites and swallow. I think she developed this unique method just so we would leave her alone.

She was still crippled in her hind legs, but she did have some use of them, so I thought it best to let her be, now that she could feed herself. Two more weeks passed and her hind legs did not improve, but she was gaining weight and keeping every extra bit of paper or cloth bedding she could stash at the very back of her cage.

I should have caught on, but sometimes we don't realize the obvious.

She had been with us for almost a month when one morning, I went to clean her cage and found two naked, pink and lifeless baby squirrels, perfectly cleaned and placed neatly just inside the door. There was also one slightly larger, very noisy and very much alive baby nursing on his mom. Mother squirrel, in spite of injured legs, missing fur and just a hint of a tilt to her head, had given birth sometime during the night. She had offered up the two deceased babies to be disposed of. She had no other way to remove them from her nest, yet she knew she had to keep her healthy baby clean and safe.

I took the two babies away and gave the new mother some clean t-shirts, which she quickly grasped in her mouth and took to the back of her cage. As the weeks passed, I marveled at how this animal managed to make the best of what for her was a truly bad situation. Each day, she cleaned and nursed her baby, watching over him as if she were completely healthy and free. She would chatter if any of us came too close to the actual nest, but she readily took the food we offered and was even beginning to climb on some of the small oak limbs we placed in her cage. I was certain that both she and her baby would be able to be set free in the not-too-distant future. But

not before our remarkable mother took on one more challenge.

Late one night, a young woman came to the Sanctuary. Her cat had brought her a newborn squirrel, barely bigger than an embryo, with his umbilical cord still attached. She could not find the nest or the mom, so she thought we might have a surrogate mother squirrel who would care for this baby. Giving an orphan to any adoptive mother is always risky. Knowing what our injured squirrel had been through, I wasn't at all sure she'd go along with our plan. I knew this pinkie baby had little hope without a real mother. He probably hadn't had very much mother's milk, and he had been carried around in a cat's mouth. It is rare for a baby with this history to survive in captivity. All we could do was hope, and make a valiant attempt to bring the two together.

I wrapped the new baby in a piece of clean t-shirt—I knew this was the mom's favorite bedding—and placed him just inside the door where she had left her two babies before. For one endless hour, nothing happened. She knew he was there because he started to squirm and cry. I began to rethink our plan. Maybe this was not such a good idea after all. Two hours passed, and I decided to pull the baby out and do what we could for him. I slowly opened the cage door. As I reached for the orphan, out of the back of the cage came the fierce chatter of a mother protecting her baby. But it was not her own baby she was chattering about. It was the little pink orphan she wanted. Our remarkable mother squirrel raced to the front of the cage and before I could grasp the motherless baby, she took him up in her mouth so gently, so quickly, telling me in no uncertain terms that this was now her baby and she'd take over from here. And take over she did.

Both babies thrived in her care. They grew fat, healthy and wild. By early summer, we were able to release the entire family. On a warm morning in May, I took the three squirrels to our release site. We placed them in a large outdoor cage and within one week, set them free. The remarkable, once-crippled mother squirrel raced out of the cage first. Finding it safe for her babies, she sat on a limb and chattered for them to join her. It was the babies' first encounter with freedom. As they chased each other through the treetops they could now call home, I was certain that the memories of their months in captivity faded quickly. Those memories were now replaced by the day-to-day joys of living with the sky overhead, the earth below and not a cage in sight.

27

The Two Herons

Our Florine Loeffler Waterbird Sanctuary Pond and island, in the midst of WRR's acres, is one of our most sensitive habitats. Originally, the island became the perfect resting spot for herons, ducks, coots, pelicans, grebes and egrets whose flight had been impaired for one reason or another. These fragile birds were given the medical attention they needed, then released onto the island and pond, free to fly away. Or, if they chose, they could continue living at the Sanctuary where free meals are provided twenty-four hours a day.

Most of the birds decide to make the pond their home for quite awhile. Some time ago, we released an adult great blue heron who had come to us with a severely bruised shoulder. Fortunately, no bones had been broken. He simply needed some time and a few free lunches to get back on his feet. When the day finally came that he was fully recovered, he flew effortlessly into the air, circled the pond gracefully several times and disappeared over the hills. We were all relieved that he

had survived his ordeal. We hoped, as we always do, that he would remain in the area and return to the pond to fish.

Weeks passed with no trace of the huge blue and gray bird. Then, one of those perfect moments occurred very early on a summer morning. The sun had been up only a short while and the Sanctuary was still quiet. As I looked out at the pond through the kitchen window, there—wading cautiously into the shallows—was a familiar figure. Those tall straight legs and the long, sleek, soft neck of that once-captive bird, extended gracefully as he strode through the water. At first, I thought he was back just to take advantage of the abundant supply of fish in the pond. But, as I continued to watch, I noticed he didn't seem interested in fishing. Several of the resident ducks floated by, quacking and splashing, but he ignored their rowdy behavior. He seemed to be waiting for something. Or, as it turned out, someone.

Only a few more minutes went by before there, in the morning sky, appeared the mate our heron was waiting for.

The female heron wasn't as confident as the male. She circled the pond several times before landing beside him. Once the two birds were side by side, they began to search through the shallow water. It wasn't long before they found enough food for a satisfying breakfast. The herons lingered on the banks of the pond for most of the morning, wading and fishing and perhaps just getting acquainted with the area. When they finally flew into the sky together, above the same hill the single heron had once before disappeared over, I knew we would be seeing these two majestic birds often. Our once-crippled great blue heron had gone back to his world, found a mate and brought her back to a place they would share in peace. Now, we look forward every year as the herons return to the pond, their second home.

28
The Mocker Takes a Sparrow

When Spring finally comes to South Texas, the baby orphaned opossums have been finding their way to the Sanctuary since February—their mothers killed on highways, shot with pellet guns, or trapped in unwelcoming backyards. The baby squirrels follow close behind: their nests torn down from treetops, the mother squirrels caught and killed by dogs and cats. Then, the first tiny, pink, fragile and featherless baby birds appear, as people get out their chainsaws and tree pruning equipment.

Each year, we rescue well over 2000 native birds. Most of these are helpless babies, each one a miracle. One of these miracle babies came to us with little or no hope for survival, but he was fortunate enough to find a surrogate mother.

A couple had been watching a family of mockingbirds build a nest in the backyard, lay their eggs and begin raising their youngsters. One tragedy after another struck the bird family. One day, father bird simply did not return to the nest. Mama mocker continued to care for her newly hatched twins, but then one was found dead on the ground. A few days later, the other baby bird followed. Finally, late one afternoon, the couple's cat caught and mauled the mama. WRR became involved when the couple brought us the injured, widowed and now childless mockingbird. She was depressed, had a severely bruised wing and one leg that was broken almost in two.

The very same day, we also received what seemed to me the world's tiniest, most naked baby sparrow. He still had bits of eggshell on his minuscule head. He must have spent only hours in his parents' care. I held out little hope for his survival.

This hatchling sparrow arrived cold and damp. He showed little interest in eating. Our first challenge was to warm him and provide small portions of fresh formula every half hour. His thin neck would barely support his head. He sat in his makeshift nest, drooping and tired, ready to give up. There was only one option left for saving the sparrow's life. I knew it was a long shot, but it was worth a try. If my plan worked, we had little to lose and so much to gain.

I placed the pink hatchling in soft tissue in the bottom of a shallow, round dish. Then, cautiously, I introduced the mama mockingbird to the orphan. He was so small that I hoped she would not mistake him for lunch. She hopped over to the dish that cradled the tiny bird, peered into it, pecked at the tissue and hopped away.

We left the baby, nest and all, in her cage. We continued to feed him, but he grew weaker. When nothing changed after two hours, it was time to try a new tactic. Knowing that mockingbirds love meal worms, we placed three large, juicy meal worms in the nest with the sparrow. Mama mocker quickly began digging around in the tissue to catch the worms. The young sparrow knew a mother bird was nearby, and began

cheeping. That did the trick. Mama mocker couldn't resist the urge to feed this little guy. It had not been so very long ago that her own babies were cheeping and begging for food. We were thrilled and hopeful. If only we could count on this pair to get along for several weeks, both their chances for survival would improve.

Things worked out better than we could have hoped. Three days after she began feeding the sparrow, the mockingbird decided to officially adopt the orphaned bird. She began to clean out his nest several times a day and, once we increased the size of the dish, she began sitting on the nest. In a matter of weeks, the baby sparrow was growing into a fully feathered youngster. He would perch on the side of the dish while his new mother perched on one of the branches in the cage. The surrogate mom was doing better as well. Once we removed the splint, we could see that her leg had mended. It was a little crooked but still very useful. Her wing was once again strong and good as new. And, she had a new family.

By the end of the following month, both birds were fat and healthy. Now came the real test. Would the mockingbird teach this baby of another species how to catch his own food? We moved the pair into a large outdoor cage and filled it with branches and soft brown leaves. There were plenty of challenges. If the baby was to learn how to hunt, he would have to learn on Mama mocker's terms.

We scattered meal worms on the leafy floor. In addition to his bowl of seed, meal worms were a primary part of the sparrow's diet. As the once-orphaned hatchling watched his mother investigate the contents of the thick leaves, he could not help but follow. He was curious about her enthusiasm and wondered what was so great about those leaves.

Finally, his mama's head surfaced. In her beak was the biggest, fastest moving worm he had ever seen. All the worms she had fed him up to now were dead. This one was very much alive. The mockingbird hopped toward the sparrow, who jumped back at least six paces! Mama mocker persisted, determined to teach him how to find live food. For several days, Mom worked diligently to instruct her adopted youngster how to take care of himself. He wanted to be fed like a baby. She wanted him to show some independence. As usual, the parent won. In no time, the sparrow was hopping about the cage, catching his own food and looking quite proud of himself.

Now came the big day. It was time to set this amazing team free. The release site was a perfect spot—lots of tall leafy trees, a pond, and acres of soft grass. We put the birds' carrier on a log. It was only moments before the mockingbird shot out of the cage and into the bright blue sky. The little sparrow was not so confident. He had never flown in the real world before.

He was not at all sure he wanted to start now, with his mother nowhere in sight.

After a long wait, the small brown and black bird peeked out of the carrier door and ventured onto the log. The world must have looked enormous to him. He had such a rough start in life, with all of his time spent in the confines of a cage. Now, there was no end in sight to the world around him. He seemed so tiny and so scared. He cheeped and cheeped, but Mama didn't come to his aid. Where was she? She had always been so near. He hopped to the very end of the huge log, calling out again and again.

Then, out of that great expanse of blue sky, who should magically appear but Mama! And she was not alone. In her beak was a huge grasshopper. What followed was a repeat performance of the sparrow's first live meal in the cage. Catching sight of the grasshopper, he jumped back in disbelief. But he rallied quickly. Mom was back with lunch and he was happy again.

After a hearty meal, Mama mocker knew it was time to teach her youngster about the world according to birds. There were trees to investigate, there was bark to peck at and there was grass to explore for the communities of insects living there. There were berries and seeds to eat and songs to learn. Best of all, there was flight. The mockingbird soared up into the tall oak tree, then called and called to her baby until he could no longer resist her coaxing. In one great, brave leap, the sparrow left the log, and his life of confinement, behind him. He was free at last. Free to fly through the air, play amongst the tree branches, hunt for food and live the life of a real, true bird, thanks to the care and nurturing of an adoptive mother not even the same species as he.

Hansel
and Gretel

We received a call one morning from a young woman named Kate, who had just moved to the outskirts of Fredericksburg, Texas, with her husband and two young children. They had purchased 200 acres of land with a pond and a great old rock cottage.

One of the first tasks she wanted to accomplish was to establish the area as a natural wildlife refuge, a place where the native animals could feel safe, and be free to come and go. We discussed various methods of attracting wild birds, squirrels, raccoons, skunks and, of course, the beautiful Hill Country deer. I gave her a list of the various types of food these animals enjoy: wild bird seed, ears of fresh corn for the squirrels, cranberries, slices of whole wheat bread, chunks of red and green apples, bananas, wild persimmons, and grapes for opossums, raccoons, skunks, and others, and mineral blocks and slices of pears for the deer.

She agreed to begin providing small amounts of all the treats —not too much of any one thing and not so much that the animals would become dependent on her for their survival.

Several weeks passed before I heard from Kate again. Then, early one morning, she called. She was very excited about having seen one of the resident does with twin fawns. She said the babies were tiny and perfect. They were sure to stay close to Mom when they weren't sleeping in the tall green grass that was their home. Kate wanted to know if she should supply any extra food for the youngsters, and I told her it was best not to change the feeding schedule, assuring her that Mom deer knew best how to care for her new twins. There was no reason to intervene. It seemed that all was well with the new family. Only days later, I learned that this was not true.

The call came around midnight. The mother doe had been seen with one fawn, but the other was nowhere to be found. Everyone was pretty sure that the twins were one male and one female. It appeared that the little future buck was doing well and the little doe fawn was the one in trouble.

We waited until morning to take action. By dawn, we were to learn exactly what the problem was. When the female fawn reappeared with her mom and brother, there was no sign of blood and no reason to think she had been injured. From a distance, all we could determine was that she had been born with a birth "defect," a withered leg, or—as we decided to refer to it—her physical challenge in life.

Kate's two children were particularly upset about the little fawn they called Gretel. Her brother, of course, was Hansel. Everyone wanted to bring Gretel into the house, make her a bed and keep her safe. After some discussion, we all agreed the very best thing to do was to let her continue to live with her family. We did decide to set up a special three-sided shed with hay, just in case Gretel ever got into trouble and needed a place to rest.

As the weeks passed, Gretel became weaker. Some days, she would appear with her mother and other days she would not. It was difficult for us to continue to do nothing, but unless she became so incapacitated that she couldn't walk, there would be no way for us even to capture her in order to help her. Little did we know that her mother was having the same thoughts.

One evening, little Gretel appeared, walking very slowly behind Mom and her big brother. The doe would stop and wait for her to catch up, which she did with great difficulty.

As they drew closer and closer to the house, the mother deer did an amazing thing. She gently nudged Gretel over to the hay bed that Kate's two children had prepared. She stayed very near, watching as her little fawn with the withered leg struggled to lie down comfortably in her warm bed. Then, quietly, the doe and Hansel walked away, back into the tall grass, back into the safety of their world.

When I arrived at the rock cottage, I was afraid Mother Nature had already made up her mind about the little fawn and that all I would be able to do was to help make Kate and her family understand why these things happen. I was in for a surprise.

Little Gretel was definitely weak, and her leg was of no use to her. But she was full of spirit and courage and had no intention of dying. She let me give her injections of fluids, and she readily nursed from a bottle full of warm fawn formula with vitamins. At first, I had every intention of bringing her back to the Sanctuary, but I soon realized that she was in the best place she could be, near her true family and in the company of a human family who was willing to feed her and keep a close eye on her.

I left Kate with strict instructions that she alone was to be the caretaker of the little fawn. Her children could not treat Gretel like a pet, because if she survived, it would be too confusing for her, once she grew up, to tell the difference between friendly humans and not-so-friendly humans.

All was set for the next twenty-four hours. There was to be a constant watch from a distance, and Gretel was to be given warm formula every three to four hours.

That same night, well after dark, when Kate went out to feed the fawn, she was met with a sight she will never forget. The mother doe and her reunited twins were all lying nestled together in the bed of warm hay. As the surrogate human mother approached, the deer family froze. Slowly Kate backed away and returned to her house. Mom, Hansel and Gretel stayed the night in the safety of their shelter. In the morning, the mother and the little male left the female fawn once again in the care of her new part-time family.

They repeated this ritual for four days. On day five, Gretel emerged from the shelter. Her withered leg was dried and small, but the rest of her was strong and her tiny fawn tummy was round and full. She cried out for over an hour, wondering where her mom and brother were. Finally, quietly and gently, as only a mother can, Mama doe came to her, licked her all over, let her nurse with her brother, looked towards the humans' house as if to say "Thank You," then took her once-again-complete family back into the tall grass, back into the safety of their own world. I am sure that the fawn known once as Gretel lived a long and healthy life, and to this day her children and her grandchildren roam through the tall grasses in the Texas Hill Country.

His Brother's Keeper

Our mild winters and abundant rains ordinarily assist Mother Nature in producing some early bouncing baby birds, squirrels, opossums and cotton-tailed rabbits. This is also the time of year when we bid a bittersweet good-bye to some remaining orphans who have come to us late in the past year to winter over at the Sanctuary. One year, the raccoon brothers were two of these. One was very tiny and the other only slightly bigger. They had been found in the wall of a house that belonged, fortunately, to Wildlife Rescue members.

The mother of the two babies had been able to carry all her other little ones out, but the two boys had slipped down between the walls outside Mom's reach. After many nights of mother and babies calling to one another, the mother raccoon had to move on and save the rest of her family.

The human family heard the cries of the tiny babies late one Tuesday evening near the fireplace and thought they might be the sounds of chimney swifts, who often build their nests

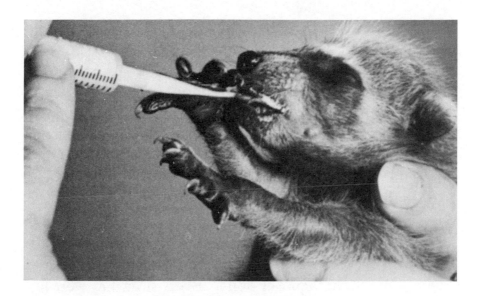

on the cool rock walls of chimneys. When the eggs hatch and the new baby birds wiggle successfully free of their shell, the shrill chirping begins.

When the cries grew louder and more persistent, it became obvious that the babies weren't newly hatched birds, but young mammals in trouble. The rescue began around 3:00 A.M. Our dedicated members took all the pictures off the wall and listened closely to determine exactly where the animals were. Once the spot was located, they very carefully began to saw around the area, taking great care not to injure the trapped animals, who now sounded like an entire litter! After almost three hours of tedious sawing and careful listening, there in the middle of two wooden beams and a great deal of sawdust sat two of the cutest, hungriest, most frightened baby raccoons anyone had ever rescued. They were cold and shivering, having been in the wall without their mom for at least three days.

Their rescuers wrapped them in warm blankets and placed them in a large cardboard box with three hot water bottles.

One call to WRR and a volunteer was on her way, baby bottle and formula in hand. When the volunteer returned to the Sanctuary with the raccoon brothers, it was easy for the staff member to see that the babies would need intensive care for several days before we could be certain they would survive. Volunteers and a staff member kept close watch, giving constant warmth, nourishment and care.

As the two grew stronger and were completely out of danger, I began to understand why they had survived their ordeal. These two amazing babies had such an incredible will to live and shared a simple devotion to one another. During the months they spent in our care, the bigger brother always watched out for his younger sibling. Every time they were fed, big brother would wait until the small one had his fill. They were inseparable at play time, scurrying up into the tree limbs in their enclosure, one encouraging the other to climb to the very top. They never stopped looking to each other for companionship and support. As the months passed, the raccoon brothers grew into independent, young adults, no longer in need of our help.

I picked the perfect release site for them, on private property along the Guadalupe River, dense with huge old cypress trees. Honeysuckle vines and four-o'clocks were blooming everywhere. Our six-foot tall, eight-foot long enclosure was on the site. It was full of tree limbs, with two sleeping boxes, a huge water trough and a feeding station. The raccoons would live there for three weeks before being set free. They were a little over half grown by now and wanted nothing to do with me. They were catching live crickets, cracking whole eggs and shelling their fill of pecans. I could still tell them apart. Every night when I'd check on them, there would be the two brothers—one big, one not so big—sticking close to each other, climbing all over the release enclosure, peering out at the old trees, listening intently to the river rushing by and smelling their new surroundings. Finally the time came to let them go.

Late one evening, I opened their door, filled their pans full of fresh fruits, nuts and chicken and stood in the shadows to watch. I wasn't surprised to see big brother come out first. He took off like a shot, ran up the nearest tree and proceeded to bound from limb to limb throughout the treetops. It took him almost fifteen minutes to realize he was alone. There, still in the doorway of the enclosure, sat his little brother, cautious as ever, and not about to budge on his own. True to their family tradition, the bigger raccoon came down from the tree, collected his brother and together they went exploring on their first night as free-roaming raccoons.

I returned faithfully each night for about six weeks to be sure that the raccoon boys had food if they needed it. I saw them on only two occasions. Both times, they were high up in the trees. All seemed to be well. The raccoons weren't coming around for their supplemental food, but I thought I would put it out for a little while longer. One evening when I went to the release site, I noticed someone sleeping in one of the wooden boxes. A closer look revealed one male raccoon. I recognized him as big brother. There was definitely something wrong. His

head was tilted to the right and when I tried to touch him, he didn't resist. As I picked him up, I could feel that he was burning with fever. As I wrapped him in my jacket, he cried out in pain. I knew that he had come back because he needed help, and as I took

him back to the Sanctuary, I wondered where his little brother was.

The following morning at the veterinarian's, we found that he had an abscess in his inner ear. If he had not come back to the site, it could have ruptured and caused serious damage. Fortunately, he wouldn't have to stay at the clinic. He needed several days' worth of medication, and I could give him that in the enclosure. The next night, I took him back to the release site, put bedding in his sleeping box and returned him to his enclosure. As I began to walk away, I heard some faint cries, so I went back to check on him. But big brother was sleeping quietly; he had not cried out at all. I heard the whimpering again, coming from the top of the tall cypress trees.

There, at the very top of a huge old tree sat the devoted little brother raccoon. He had probably been watching as I took big brother away the night before. Now it was the younger brother who was the caretaker. Five nights he waited. Finally on the sixth night, when the enclosure door was opened and big brother once again climbed exuberantly back into the treetops, there, waiting patiently, was his little brother.

I still see the raccoon boys every so often, in their favorite place among the treetops, far from reach.

Once more, their life is their own. The two raccoons, together again, have reclaimed their place in Nature, playing in the treetops, hunting along the banks of the river and living out their lives as free wild animals.

31 The Dove Family and the Dog

It's always interesting to follow the path of an animal who finds himself in trouble. It is particularly interesting when you never actually meet the animal—or person—who brings the plight to your attention. This usually happens most frequently during baby season.

The most memorable of these was a call from an elderly woman who had been closely watching a mother and father dove. The pair had constructed a nest in the honeysuckle vines just outside her bedroom window. Early each morning, the mother dove would awaken the woman with her soft cooing. The bird had been persistently sitting on her nest for what seemed, to the woman, a long time. One morning, there were two tiny, shaky heads peeking out from under the mother's wings. The woman described the babies as small and frail, with large beaks and wiry hair.

Doves' nests are quite fragile. All too often, as the babies grow, the nest is not substantial enough to hold them. These two babies, however, seemed to be doing fine. The trouble had started one afternoon when the woman noticed a large dog sniffing around the vines. Concerned that the dog meant the dove family harm, the caller asked if she should risk moving the nest to a safer area. I told her that even though they were at risk, it was almost certain death if the babies, nest and all, were removed. Usually, birds will accept their young being placed back in the nest or in a box *if* the nest or babies have fallen out of the tree. But they have an altogether different reaction if someone actually takes the nest away.

We agreed that she should leave the nest and keep an eye out for the dog. I also suggested she try to locate the dog's people so they could keep her in for a while. After combing the neighborhood, the woman could find no one who would claim the dog. Days passed without incident. The dog would come by in the late afternoon. She was a large yellow dog of mixed heritage and seemed quite gentle, but we decided to keep an eye on her nonetheless.

The baby doves grew in size and strength. Their parents continued to feed and care for them, watching their every move as they grew too large for their tiny nest. One afternoon, while Mom and Dad Dove were gone (no doubt lunching at a local bird feeder), the woman looked out to check on the two baby doves. She was alarmed to find only one in the nest. They were not yet big enough to leave, so she assumed the worst had happened. Just as she was about to go outside to look for the missing fledgling, she witnessed an amazing sight.

Under the nest, there sat a large gray cat. Just above him, still in the cover of the honeysuckle vines, was the missing baby dove. Apparently, he had left the safety of the nest and traveled a few feet away into the vines. The cat had no doubt been attracted by the baby's fluttering in the thick foliage.

Being true to his feline nature, the cat was beginning his ascent into the honeysuckle, when who should appear but the large yellow dog. She began barking at the cat, who froze in place. The woman watched in awe as the big, yellow dog stood her ground, barking persistently until the cat gathered his wits and fled from the woman's yard. Quietly, the dog lay down beneath the nest.

It was only minutes before the parents returned. One went to the baby in the vines while the other returned to the nest to sit with the remaining fledgling. Once the family was re-united, their friend the dog again disappeared. Whether Mom and Dad Dove knew what had taken place, we'll never know. And when the two young doves had grown and left the nest with Mom and Dad, our caller never saw them again. Nor did she see the big, gentle, yellow dog again.

I guess if I were ever asked if I believe in angels, after all these years of working with animals and people doing their best to survive and help others survive, I would have to say that I can't *help* but believe in angels. And after working with the dear woman who cared so much about those doves, and hearing her story about the little miracle in her own back- yard, I have to see her and the dog as angels here on earth.